INSPIRING
YOUNG AUTHORS
YEAR-ROUND

Enjoy bookmaking!

Nancy Steffel

Susie Swensen

2-10-90

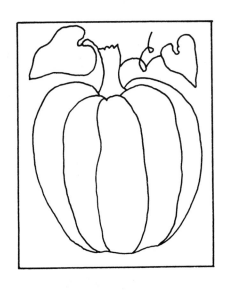

Inspiring
Young Authors
Year-Round

A Handbook
for Teachers and Parents

By Nancy Oster Steffel, Ed. D.,
and
Susan Griffis Swenson, M.S. Ed.

Illustrated by Elizabeth Cameron Evans

Treetop Publishing   Racine, Wisconsin

Library of Congress Catalog Number: 89-51205

ISBN 0-9623378-0-3 (Library Edition)

ISBN 0-9623378-1-1 (Paperback Edition)

The artwork on pages 127, 128, 141 and 142
was drawn by various artists.

Printed and bound in the United States of America

Contents

Acknowledgment

We want to thank
Gene Dodd for asking us to write this book,
Donna Stephenson for listening to our shared readings,
and our families for understanding our need to make books.

Preface

''We're bookmakers!'' we answer proudly whenever people ask us what we do.

''Bookmakers?'' they respond with raised eyebrows and skewed grins, obviously considering the shadier connotation of the word.

''Yes, we create books based on our personal experiences, favorite songs, and creative ideas.''

''Have you had any published?'' they inquire curiously.

''Yes, self-published,'' we explain and show them one of our books written in a blank (Bare) book.

''But this is bound and looks like a real book!'' they marvel.

We smile coyly. ''Fortunately, we don't have to bind our books. We just make up the stories and pictures.''

''How many have you written?'' they then ask.

''Around a hundred between our two families. But we have ideas for hundreds more books that we would like to make. In fact, we have enough ideas to write a book about them!''

And so we decided to do just that. This book represents all the books we have made or would love to make.

Introduction

Many of you, as teachers and parents, may already encourage your children to write books as part of an annual young authors' program. How about inspiring young authors to create books all through the year? After working with preschool and elementary school children of various capabilities, we have found bookmaking to be one of the most effective strategies to help children grow as readers and writers. Here are ten reasons to incorporate bookmaking as a year-round experience in your school's curriculum or your family's activities:

1. **Bookmaking provides personalized writing opportunities.** As authors, children can create and express ideas based on their personal experiences and language abilities. They can apply grammar lessons and other language conventions in their own writing rather than on one worksheet exercise given to an entire class. Teachers and parents have shared stories with us about children who would not write stories until they had the opportunity to write books about *themselves* — their experiences, their interests, and their desires.

2. **Bookmaking supplies writers with audiences.** If children are to learn to communicate their ideas in writing, they must know that others will read their work. As an elementary student in the 1950s and 1960s, Nancy remembers writing for three audiences: her mother, the teacher, and the bulletin board. The first copy was completed in pencil for her mother to

read and edit. Then she carefully wrote the second copy in ink for her teacher to read and correct. Occasionally, Nancy had to produce a third copy in her best handwriting to be displayed on the bulletin board. Since the students were not allowed to get out of their seats during class, the intended reader of her third effort must have been the bulletin board. By making books, children are assured of a reading audience because their books can be shared with others both in the classroom and at home.

3. **Bookmaking realistically involves the revision and editing processes.** Writing involves more than the pencil and ink drafts described in the above anecdote. Interviews with authors and illustrators reveal that they make numerous drafts of their stories as they try to create the best possible texts and illustrations. Bookmaking supplies a context in which students learn the process of revision. Children are often more willing to invest time in rewriting their work if it is for a book rather than just for the sake of producing a perfect paper.

4. **Bookmaking offers a familiar structure of writing.** "For Better or For Worse" cartoonist Lynn Johnston (*It Must Be Nice to Be Little,* p. 94) illustrates a writing dilemma with a mother examining her son's homework. The concerned mother exclaims that his one-sentence text is not the short story the teacher assigned him to write. The discouraged son replies that he couldn't make it any shorter! Most children are exposed to books from an early age and become familiar with a book's organization. Thus, creating books can be a familiar process for children than writing a short story or paragraph.

5. **Bookmaking provides a meaningful writing situation.** Children's familiarity with the purposes and structures of books is essential to ensure their involvement and success in writing. Jim Trelease, author of *The Read Aloud Handbook,* remarked in a presentation to parents and teachers that most young adults learn to drive rather easily. He explained that after children have ridden in the car for sixteen years, they know the car's use and value to them. The same principle can be transferred: children who are familiar with books as listeners and readers will want to be authors because they are aware of the purposes and the values of writing books.

6. **Bookmaking integrates reading and writing.** As collaborators on this book, we each had to write with the reader in mind. Exchanging copy, we then had to read to determine what our partner was trying to say. In other words, we had to write as readers and read as writers. It is important that children learn this writing-reading process to assist them to communicate more effectively through print. This learning can be achieved through bookmaking in which the children are involved in roles both as readers and as writers.

7. **Bookmaking supplies personalized reading materials**. A book written by a child can describe his or her experiences or ideas in a way that no other book can because it contains the child's own thoughts, language, and art. Books created by teachers and parents can teach new concepts by connecting children's personal backgrounds with the information presented. These personalized books offer more predictable, and thus easier, reading materials for children — the content meets the readers' prior experiences, knowledge, and language abilities.

8. **Bookmaking provides communication**. A book describing personal experiences and family activities can help others to learn about the author's home life. Books created about school schedules, classmates, and special events can inform parents and new students about the learning environment. In a simple, nonthreatening manner, these books can help individuals to share information that will foster closer cooperation and better understanding.

9. **Bookmaking creates cherished keepsakes**. Teachers, parents, and children can express their love and appreciation to friends and relatives by creating special editions for their libraries. These books record memories that can be relived as the books are read. A child-made book provides a record of a child's language and artistic abilities at a particular age. Also, people young or old feel a special satisfaction when they create or receive a book, a gift that can be enjoyed again and again. Even if a homemade book was given for a past holiday, a new book can be designed on a different topic or with new information.

10. **Bookmaking is fun and rewarding**. As we design pages, supply illustrations, and write text, we fulfill our creative urges. Often we find ourselves staying up till the wee hours rhyming words to create a rhythmic text to accompany family snapshots of a vacation or a birthday party. Why? Because bookmaking is fun! We feel a special pride when we finish a book and share it with others. Children should also have an opportunity to write recreationally, for their own satisfaction and not always for report card grades. They should have the opportunity to enjoy authorship more than once a year. Imagine the personal library children would have if they could make a book each month of the year.

We hope that our book will inspire you, and that in turn, you will inspire children, to become bookmakers — authors, illustrators, designers, and publishers. The first section presents suggestions, tips, and techniques for implementing bookmaking in your school or home activities with children. The second section offers ideas, arranged thematically, for making books from September through summer. Sources of materials mentioned and sample forms are supplied at the end of the book.

Section

1

Guidelines for Inspiring Young Authors

Teachers and parents have asked us how they can assist children to create books. In reply, we developed the following guidelines for inspiring young authors. We feel it important that children be provided with:

A An Appropriate Anticipatory Activity

B Benefit of Both Book Writing and Book Reading

C Chances and Choices for Publication

D Developing the Desire to Read and Write

E Energetic, Enthusiastic Examples

By following the suggestions presented in this section, parents and teachers will encourage children to become active authors, illustrators, readers, and — most importantly — learners.

Chapter 1

An Appropriate Anticipatory Activity

Before writing, a writer must anticipate what he or she will be writing about. This advance thinking serves as a rehearsal for the initial writing and a time for sorting information and ideas needed for the writing. Illustrators and book designers use this same process.

Teachers and parents can help children prepare to write by providing opportunities for them to recall their background experiences and knowledge, acquire more information and details, and observe writing patterns and samples. This chapter presents ideas for assisting young bookmakers with these preliminary steps.

RECALLING BACKGROUND EXPERIENCES AND KNOWLEDGE

If you ask writers and illustrators the sources for their ideas, they will answer that they rely on past experiences and apply previous knowledge in their work. As teachers and parents, you can captivate students' interests, activate their memories, and stimulate their imaginations by utilizing one or a combination of the following prewriting strategies.

Guided Imagery

Through this strategy, students can mentally explore an experience narrated to them. A teacher or a parent structures a situation and then prompts each child to recall background experiences and knowledge. You can help students paint a mental picture as a preparation for writing or drawing. For example, slowly read a paragraph such as the following, pausing to allow your young listeners to think about each dimension.

Close your eyes. Pretend it is the morning of your next birthday, and you have just awakened. You lie in bed, thinking about the special day to come. You know that this will be the best birthday ever because you are having a party. You think about who is coming to your party...what you might receive for gifts...what food will be served...where the party will be held...what activities are planned. Soon it is time for the party to begin. There are lots of decorations and friends start arriving for the party. Now open your eyes. Write a story and draw pictures about your best birthday ever.

Conceptually Related Reading

Writers can benefit by reading or hearing books, stories, poems, or songs on the same topic they plan to write about. This helps students to begin thinking about their writing assignment and to organize their thoughts. For instance, to prepare students to write about grandparents, a teacher might play the song "Grandmas and Grandpas" by Katrina Butler on the album *Deep in the Forest* by Joe Scruggs, and then read the books *I Have Four Names for My Grandfather* by Kathryn Lasky and *I Know a Lady* by Charlotte Zolotow. Afterward, the teacher could encourage the students to share their ideas by asking questions:

What name or names do you have for your grandfather or grandmother?

If you don't have grandparents living, what other older persons are special to you?

What do you like to do together with your grandparent or older person?

Brainstorming

Teachers and parents can assist children in generating ideas for writing through brainstorming related experiences, specific concepts, or technical vocabulary. Students can individually jot down their ideas in lists on paper, and then collectively share those ideas, which can be recorded by the teacher on the blackboard, an overhead projector, or chart paper. The ideas generated can be categorized or sequenced for the students' writing needs. For example, if the children were to write about their last dental checkups, they might list:

Dentist	Teeth	Floride
Hygienist	Tongue	X-ray
Appointment	Toothbrush	Rinse mouth
Waiting room	Floss	Cleaned teeth
Dental chair	Cavity	New filling

Clustering, Semantic Webbing, Mapping, or Charting

Students can draw or write their ideas in arrays, pictures, or charts. In these diagrams, they can note key points and supporting details, or they can plot out sequences of events or ideas. Using the information they have outlined, the students can then design their books. Demonstrated below are an array, a picture outline, and a chart for the story of the "Three Honey Bees and the Big Bear" (similar to "Three Billy Goats Gruff").

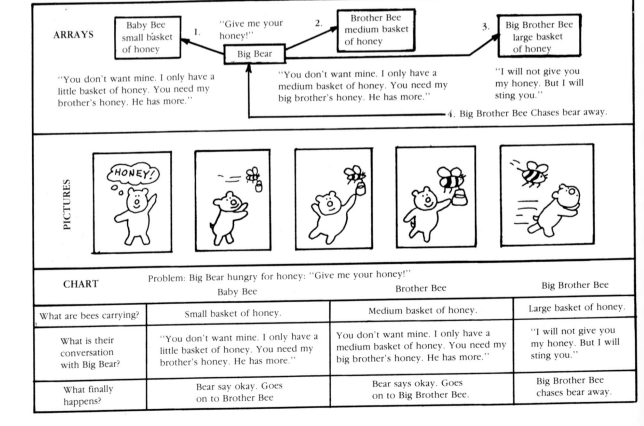

Free Writing/Free Drawing

Children should have opportunities to write or draw about self-selected topics. In journals or on scratch paper, they can record new impressions, interesting observations, or favorite expressions. Students need time to ponder problems, clarify thoughts, and generate new ideas. Through their writing, they also can begin to analyze their feelings and evaluate experiences. Spontaneous writing or drawing engages students' thinking to create text and/or pictures without worrying about form or correctness. After samples of free writing and free drawing accumulate in their journals or writing folders, the students can rewrite or redraw these initial drafts.

ACQUIRING MORE INFORMATION AND DETAILS

To begin any writing assignment, writers must consider what information is needed. Writers must collect all their thoughts and experiences on the topic to see what they already know. Then they determine what information they still need to gather. To help children with this inquiry process, teachers and parents need to guide young writers and illustrators to develop questions, plan interviews, and conduct research. These three steps can be demonstrated using the example of a little girl writing about her pet dog.

Questioning

Initially, seven-year-old Mary sat down and wrote out what she knew about her dog Nutmeg:

> Nutmeg is a dachshund and she is fourteen years old.
> She likes dog cookies and to play ball.
> Everyday we feed her dog food and give her water.
> She can do tricks like roll over and sit up.

She showed her brief story to her mom and asked her to get pictures out of their photo album to help illustrate her story. As her mom went to get the pictures, Mary began to think of questions to ask:

When did you get Nutmeg?
Why did you get her?
Who named her?
What was she like when she was little?
How did you train her?

As seen in this example, to write thoroughly on a topic, students need to look over their initial draft to think of questions they need to ask to get more information. These questions can be listed on one sheet of paper or placed individually on separate index cards. Then the answers can be put next to each question.

Interviewing

While looking at the photos with her mom, Mary asked her questions. Through this conversation, she generated still more questions about experiences with Nutmeg over the last fourteen years. Her mom helped her write down the information so she would not forget what they discussed. Together they categorized and sequenced the photos to match her notes.

Writers can interview others to gain information to add to their background knowledge, as Mary did with her mother. The interviewing strategy is also used to gain information about individuals. For example, to learn about classmates at the beginning of school, students can interview each other to prepare a class book (see SEPTEMBER — Classmates for more details). Finally, students can learn about writing style or artistic design by interviewing a published author or illustrator. This information can be helpful to students as they attempt to assemble their ideas in words and pictures for their own books.

Researching

Mary still had questions about dachshunds, such as how long dachshunds normally live and why dachshunds have such short legs and long bodies. The next day, her teacher helped her to look in the library for a book on dogs. The book Mary found not only answered her questions, but it also told her more about dachshunds' other attributes. With all this information, Mary began to write her book, *My Dog Nutmeg*.

Young authors may want to consult reference books in the library or engage in additional background experiences, such as traveling or experimenting, to acquire the information needed to write. For instance, to write his mystery story, a boy may need to know how a mirror reflects, how a two-story house is laid out, or how a deed is written. Librarians, teachers, and parents can help the young authors as they attempt to answer their questions.

OBSERVING WRITING PATTERNS AND SAMPLES

Writers often use patterns to organize their writing. A pattern may employ a specific language, plot, or style. Teachers and parents can share with children samples that demonstrate particular patterns of writing. The young authors can then adapt the patterns for use in their own writing. Let's take the example discussed earlier about the children assigned to write about their grandparents or another important older adult. Besides preparing the young authors to write, the record and books would demonstrate to the children how other authors organize and express their ideas.

Various patterns that might assist young authors to create books are listed on the following pages. Samples that demonstrate each pattern are also given and cross-referenced with the ideas presented in Section 2.

Syntactically Repetitive Patterns

Children may want to tell their stories using the repetition of language patterns. These patterns are easy and helpful for beginning writers because they often supply the sentences to be used and require only the addition of a few words. Other patterns give sentence or paragraph structure to support the young authors in expressing ideas. Here are a variety of predictable patterns that could be used.

Counting Pattern   This pattern includes simple counting, such as in ''The Elephant Song'' (see OCTOBER — Halloween):

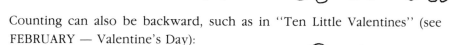

> One elephant went out to play...
> Two elephants went out to play...
> Three elephants went out to play...

Counting can also be backward, such as in ''Ten Little Valentines'' (see FEBRUARY — Valentine's Day):

> Ten little valentines...
> Nine little valentines...
> Eight little valentines...

Ordinal numbers can be used, as in ''Five Little Pumpkins'' (see OCTOBER — Halloween):

> Five little pumpkins sitting on a gate.
> The first one said...
> The second one said...

Chronological Pattern   Ideas can be presented as they occur by month, day, or hour. Here are some examples.

Month - (see MAY — Yearbooks)
> In January I'll want to share...
> In February I'll design...
> In March I'll draw...

Day - (see SEPTEMBER — School Routines)
> Monday, I'm happy to...
> Tuesday, I'm happy to...
> Wednesday, I'm happy to...

Hour - (see FEBRUARY — Dental Health Month)
> When you wake up in the morning, and
> it's quarter to one...
> ...it's quarter to two...
> ...it's quarter to three...

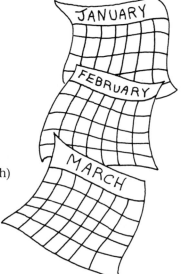

Alphabetical Pattern   Using the letters in the alphabet can provide a predictable organization for a book (see SEPTEMBER — School Routines):

A is for *a*fternoon when we...
B is for the fifteen *b*oys...
C is for...

A text can also be designed around associating the letters in the name of a person, place, or holiday with words that begin with the same letters to form an acrostic (see NOVEMBER — Friends):

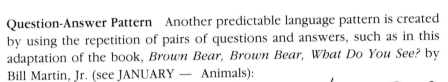

A is for *a*ll the fun...
L is for *l*unch when...
E is for the *e*normous frog...
X is for the *e*xtra time...

Question-Answer Pattern   Another predictable language pattern is created by using the repetition of pairs of questions and answers, such as in this adaptation of the book, *Brown Bear, Brown Bear, What Do You See?* by Bill Martin, Jr. (see JANUARY — Animals):

Blank ant, black ant, who do you see?
I see a yellow chick following me.
Yellow chick, yellow chick, who do you see?
I see a red hen following me.

Verse-Refrain Pattern   Poems and songs use this pattern of different verses with a repeating refrain. This is illustrated in the song, ''Brush Your Teeth'' (see FEBRUARY — Dental Health Month):

When you wake up in the morning,
and it's quarter to one...
REFRAIN:
You brush your teeth — Ch, ch, ch, ch,
ch, ch, ch, ch, ch

Author-Created Patterns   In books, poems, or songs, writers can create repetitive language patterns that other authors can utilize. For instance, Sarah Hayes used the pattern of the cumulative nursery rhyme, ''The House That Jack Built'' to tell a story about a teddy bear's trip to the dump (see SUMMER — ''Reading Rainbow''). Some variations using the pattern created in Charlotte Zolotow's wishful book, *Someday* are suggested (see NOVEMBER — Careers and MAY — Histories):

Someday, I want to meet_____, because...
Someday, I will be a(n) _____.
Someday, I will travel to _____.
Someday, I'm going to write a book about_____.

Personalized Patterns   There are patterns that teachers and parents can design for children to use to fill in their ideas and experiences to create their own personal versions of the text. These patterns can be organized in various ways:

Fill-in Sentences (see NOVEMBER — Family):

My mom is special because _____

A favorite time with my mom was when _____

Mary

Chuck

Fill-in Paragraph (see SEPTEMBER — Classmates):

My name is_____. When I am home, two of my favorite things to do are _____ and _____.

Sarah

Fill-in Story (see OCTOBER — Halloween):

I wore a _____costume when I was one, and thought Halloween was lots of fun.

Laura

I dressed like a _____ when I was two, and was a little bit scared...

Andy

Semantic Patterns

Writers also need patterns to help them organize longer and more detailed texts. A semantic pattern presents a structure for expressing an author's message and ideas. Consider once more the example of the child writing about his or her grandparent. The young author must decide if the writing will be structured as a poem, an essay, or a biography. Here are a few sample patterns that teachers and parents can share with their children to encourage and organize their writing.

Story Pattern   Story patterns help children to tell their stories. The structure includes providing a setting for the story, creating central characters, plotting events, possibly including problems, reaching a climax, and providing an ending resolution. Some examples:

Sequel Format: Using realistic fiction or mystery books as patterns, young authors may decide to write an exciting sequel with the same main characters or recreate the story with themselves involved in the tale. They can use the original book's plot to structure their version (see MARCH — Present).

Folktale Format: Folktales are based on word-of-mouth stories that different cultures create about nature or their society. Tall tales follow this format but also include exaggerated situations. Fairy tales use a magical element to enhance the story along with the predictable beginning, "Once upon a time," and an ending, "They lived happily ever after." Children can retell a common tale or try to create a new story using one of these formats (see SUMMER — "Reading Rainbow").

Reader-Response Format: Using this pattern, a writer designs a setting and then provides two options; the reader must select one to move through the story's events toward the end. Young authors can observe this pattern in a variety of books, such as the "Choose Your Own Adventure" series with science fiction stories by Bantam Books or the "Time Traveler" series with historical fiction stories by Bantam-Skylark Books (see MARCH — Future).

Poetic Pattern   This pattern of writing has its own structures and rules for using language to create rhyme, rhythm, or form. Young authors can copy traditional (public domain) poems or create their own poetry, which they can illustrate or just place in books. Examples of poetry are used throughout Section 2.

Informational Pattern   Young authors can create factual books to provide additional information and serve as classroom or home reference books. The science, health, and social studies curricula can be supplemented with student-written books on such subjects as animals' life cycles (see APRIL — Growing), poison control (see FEBRUARY — Dental Health Month), or states (see JANUARY — Habitats).

Biographic Format: Biographies describe the attributes, experiences, and ideas of individuals who are living or have lived. Young authors can create biographies about people they have met or researched (see SEPTEMBER — Classmates and FEBRUARY — Presidents' Day).

Reference Format: Dictionaries, instructional books, and phone directories list pertinent information arranged in a specific sequence. Young authors can make these types of books to assist themselves in their daily lives (see SUMMER — Potpourri).

Writing Styles

The style of writing an author uses influences the selection, sequence, and description of events and information used in a book. The style creates the tone or mood of the writing. For instance, to write a humorous book, an author might decide to do one of the following:

Include funny anecdotes and expressions in the text, such as Beverly Cleary uses in the "Ramona Quimby" series when she describes Ramona growing up (see March — Present).

Exaggerate descriptions or experiences, such as Judith Viorst depicts in *Alexander and the Terrible, Horrible, No Good, Very Bad Day,* when everything goes wrong for a little boy one day (see MARCH — Present).

Merge different vocabulary in a specific writing pattern. For instance, Judi Barrett creates a silly tale about a land where food rains from the sky in *Cloudy With a Chance of Meatballs.* The menu for food is presented as weather forecasts (see APRIL — Weather).

Create misunderstandings when language is misinterpreted, as Peggy Parish accomplishes in her "Amelia Bedelia" series, with Amelia throwing dust over the living room when she is told to dust the furniture (see MARCH — Present).

Present events in an unpredictable fashion, such as Trinka Hakes Noble accomplishes in *The Day Jimmy's Boa Ate the Wash,* with a child's retelling of her class field trip opposite to the way the events occurred (see SEPTEMBER — Field Trips).

Add something outlandish to a "normal" situation, such as when David Small adds antlers to Imogene's head one day in his book *Imogene's Antlers* (see MARCH — Present).

Include pictures that depict a funny scene, such as Ron Barrett's drawing of a chicken wearing pants with an egg stuck in them in Judi Barrett's *Animals should definitely not wear clothing* (see JANUARY — Animals).

The list could continue with various techniques that an author could use to create a humorous mood for a story. If the author instead wanted to write in a more serious or evaluative style, a different list of options would be available. How the author intends to present the ideas on paper influences the selection and sequencing of the information. Also affected are the vocabulary and language patterns chosen for the written work.

To help children anticipate what they are going to write, teachers and parents can provide opportunities for children to see samples of different writing patterns and styles. By determining what pattern and/or style they want to use, young authors can then select what information and ideas they need to begin to write.

Chapter 2

Benefit of Both Book Writing and Book Reading

Young authors need to create a variety of pieces of writing from which a selection could be revised and edited for publication. To help them improve their ability to communicate in print, students also need to read writing produced by professional writers and school peers. By analyzing others' writing, children can better evaluate and improve their own work.

Teachers and parents can assist children by creating the time and opportunity for their young authors to write and read books. They can also provide guidance and feedback to the children. This chapter will discuss the writing process and how children can participate as authors.

WRITING AND REVISING DRAFTS

Children prepare their first drafts on paper or computer screens. This is not a difficult task because they have had time to rehearse for the experience through an anticipatory activity. They are interested and motivated to write. They have thought about what they are going to write and how they are going to say it.

First Draft

Since the purpose of the first draft is to get ideas into writing, children must not be bogged down with the form their writing takes. Their ideas can be listed, placed in sentences, or connected in paragraphs. Handwriting and other language conventions (spelling, grammar, capitalization, and punctuation) are not the priority. When the children are unsure how to phrase something or how to spell words, they can leave a space or a question mark, and move on to the next thought. Sketches or diagrams can be added to help record their ideas.

Teachers, parents, or even other children can assist young authors to get their ideas into print by scribing for them. As the child dictates his or her ideas, the scribe should try to get the main points down, using the child's language. If there are more children wanting help than there are scribes available, allow the young authors to record their stories on tape for later transcription. The tape recorder facilitates accurate scribing because the tape can be replayed as needed.

Young authors' first drafts can be placed in their writing folders or written in their creative writing journals. Each child's writing should accumulate so that the young author can reread his or her writing to select which draft will be rewritten. Children need to know that not all drafts will be revised, edited, and eventually published.

Shared Reading

When young authors are interested in refining their initial drafts, they can read their work to a group of students or to a partner. The listeners need to consider only what and how the information is presented. Concern for language mechanics will come later. The listeners need to provide feedback on how the author was effective as well as ineffective. Often an author will gain helpful insight for subsequent revisions by just reading his or her rough

draft aloud. The author can also ask the listeners' advice about rewriting his or her work.

Parents and teachers can also listen to children read their first drafts. The adults must be careful to provide suggestions without telling the children how and what to write. When working with one child, a parent or teacher can read the child's work aloud so that the child can more actively listen to his or her written ideas and determine what changes to make on the next draft.

Revision and Self-editing

By trying out their initial written ideas on an audience, young authors have a better understanding of how they need to write and what information needs to be added, deleted, or reworded. As subsequent drafts are completed, children can request additional shared readings to receive more feedback if needed.

Young authors must maintain ownership of their writing by controlling what revisions are made. Teachers and parents should suggest, not demand, changes in children's work. It is helpful for adults to remember that a child's written work is a snapshot of his or her written language development at a particular age. They should appreciate it as they would cherish a recording of their child's first spoken words.

Once the authors feel that their texts express what they intend, they can begin to edit their writing to follow language conventions and revise their wording to ensure fluency and clarity. They can seek help from an outside editor or proofreader in refining their work.

Outside Editing

Children can take turns serving as outside editors for classmates. A teacher may volunteer his or her services as well. At home, parents and older siblings can proofread a young author's work. Materials, such as a dictionary, a thesaurus, and an English stylebook, should be available for reference. Marks may be made on the paper itself, or repositionable self-adhesive notes can be used to indicate where corrections or changes are needed.

The young authors will review the comments made by the editors or proofreaders, then rewrite their texts for publication. They must keep in mind that additional rewriting may be necessary when they lay out their texts and illustrations on pages for their book. Throughout this process, they must understand that there is no good writing, just good rewriting.

For additional advice on guiding children through the writing process, consult *Creating Classrooms for Authors* by Jerome Harste and Kathy Short, with Carolyn Burke, or the parenting handbook, *Growing Up Writing* by Linda Leonard Lamme.

READING AND EVALUATING TEXTS

Children, not only learn to write by writing, but they also learn to write by reading. As budding young authors, they need to read books to discover how other authors write effectively. Teachers and parents can help by providing book discussions and writing reviews, during which children read and evaluate work written by professional writers and their school peers. By gaining insights about writing and the decisions other writers make, children can improve their own writing.

Book Discussions

A book discussion offers an opportunity for children to respond analytically to books and to share their opinions with others. Through their exchange of comments, they can deepen their understanding of literature and the writing process. Teachers can schedule book discussions as a regular event in class, and parents can include this activity occasionally during the nightly read-aloud time with their children.

Teachers and parents, with the aid of librarians, can initially choose books in a specific category for children to study. As children become familiar with book discussions, they can assume some of the responsibility of selecting the books to be analyzed. Possible categories of books for discussion include:

Books with the same author and/or illustrator, such as:
Judi Barrett
Animals should definitely not wear clothing (see JANUARY — Animals)
Cloudy With a Chance of Meatballs (see APRIL — Weather)
Pickles Have Pimples (see SUMMER — Potpourri)

Eric Carle
The Very Busy Spider (see JANUARY — Animals)
The Very Hungry Caterpillar (see APRIL — Weather)
The Secret Birthday Message (see SUMMER — Potpourri)

Books in a series, for example (see MARCH — Present)
''Ramona Quimby'' series by Beverly Cleary
''Homer Price'' series by Robert McCloskey

Books with different versions of the same tales, such as: (see SUMMER — ''Reading Rainbow'')
Paul Bunyan
Rumpelstiltskin

Books on the same theme such as a bad day: (see MARCH — Present)
Today Was a Terrible Day by Patricia Giff
Alexander and the Terrible, Horrible, No Good, Very Bad Day by Judith Viorst

Books on the same topic, for instance, spiders (see JANUARY — Animals)
  The Lady and the Spider by Faith McNulty
  Spider's Web by Christine Back and Barrie Watts

Books written by young authors can also be included in the book discussions. Children's work can be the focus of a discussion, using their rough drafts and books to evaluate their writing development and style.

To assist the children's analysis of the books chosen, several guidelines are suggested:

1. Select two or three books to be discussed.
2. Before the discussion group begins, each member should have heard or read every book in the category chosen. It is helpful for teachers to get multiple copies to allow more students access to the books.
3. Every member is encouraged to contribute ideas. If desired, a parent or teacher may also participate. Any member can be the leader.
4. It is helpful if one member takes notes, whether on paper, an overhead transparency, or a blackboard. These notes can serve as a reference for the discussion and subsequent writing.
5. Members can begin the discussion by sharing their reactions to the books, noting similarities and differences among the books, or commenting on the style of the author(s).
6. Be sure to ask members to substantiate their comments by citing what a particular author actually wrote.

To help children learn more about an author's decision-making process, filmed interviews with different professional authors can be shown. Schools can arrange to have local authors visit with students in their classes or to hold teleconferences with authors in other parts of the country. Libraries and bookstores often invite authors for programs that families can attend.

For other discussion topics and book titles, teachers can consult *Focus Units in Literature: A Handbook for Elementary School Teachers* by Joy Moss or *Children's Choices: Teaching with Books Children Like* edited by Nancy Roser and Margaret Firth. Parents can find suggestions in *A Parent's Guide to Children's Reading* by Nancy Larrick or *The Read-Aloud Book* by Jim Trelease.

Writing Reviews

During a writing review, children compare effective and ineffective writing characteristics. They summarize their findings by compiling a comparative writing guide. With this guide, they can then evaluate their own writing to determine ways to improve it. Writing reviews can occur as part of book discussion or shared reading activities when young authors are busy discussing and analyzing books and/or their written drafts.

Teachers or parents may choose to lead the writing reviews at first until the children are ready to take their turns. To design a comparative writing guide, a leader should ask the group members to brainstorm what qualities they observed in the best versus the poor work they read. A list of writing characteristics can be created that might look like the following:

An effective writer
- uses correct sentence structure and includes some sentence variation
- organizes ideas clearly and with unity
- includes descriptive vocabulary that helps the reader picture the ideas
- makes few errors in mechanics and spells most words correctly

An ineffective writer
- wanders and does not have a clear story
- has a limited word choice
- does not provide enough detail for the reader
- has run-on sentences or fragments
- makes errors in mechanics
- misspells many words

More specific traits of good writing could be noted depending on the writing structures and styles used. For example, if students were evaluating poems, they could develop a list of characteristics of good poetry. This list could serve as a guide for their writing or could be used as criteria for selecting the best poems to place in a class or personal anthology.

Using the comparative writing guide they develop, young authors can analyze their own writing to determine which good traits they exhibit. They can work to improve their writing by developing traits they need to acquire.

VARIED EXPERIENCES OF AUTHORSHIP

Children can have varied experiences with authorship by writing individually or collaboratively. Each experience with authorship provides a way for students to grow as readers, writers, and learners.

Individual Authorship

Writing individually, children have the opportunity to control how and what ideas are expressed based on their background knowledge, language abilities, and personal interests. They experience ownership for the revision and publication of their works. The completion of each book is an individual responsibility.

Children can also participate as individual authors without writing the whole book alone. They can write a page or a section for a class-made book or submit a poem or a short story for a class anthology. As contributing authors, they can enjoy being published but with less work and time required of them.

Collaborative Authorship

Writing with a partner or a group also has its advantages for authorship. As each child produces text, the partners respond to its effectiveness and assist in its revisions. The authors have the benefit of their collective experiences, knowledge, and abilities in writing their book. They can help pace each other to complete the necessary drafts for final publication. The only limitation is how compatible the authors are in working together.

Young authors can work as collaborators in groups or pairs. In school, children can write collectively with their class or reading group. They can work in pairs, with one student as the author and the other student as the illustrator. They can match up with a friend or someone with similar interests. Teachers can group children for bookmaking by placing more competent students with less able language users.

Families can also collaborate by writing books together on personal topics, such as their home, holiday traditions, or summer vacation. A parent and a child or two siblings could work together to write a personal book for a specific relative. Bookmaking provides a unique opportunity for families to work and talk together. As a result, they create lasting memories and special family keepsakes.

Children definitely need to learn to read as writers and write as readers. Through book writing and book reading, they can achieve this goal.

Chapter 3

Choices and Chances for Publication

After writers have completed the final drafts of their manuscripts, they are ready to make a variety of choices in order to publish their books. First, they must lay out the text on the pages so that their stories read well. Illustrations are then planned to correspond with their writing. Finally, the pages are assembled into book form. This chapter presents ways teachers and parents can offer choices and chances to young authors.

CHOICES FOR TEXT

As young authors lay out their text, they need to make decisions regarding text placement and typography. To help them through this process, students can make a booklet that publishers refer to as a dummy. Dummies allow young authors to rehearse the layout of text and graphics before making their final book. Teachers and parents can help students prepare dummies by stapling or sewing sheets of paper together to create pages in the sizes of the final books. Repositionable self-adhesive tape or notes allow young authors to try out different placements of text directly in blank books.

After a dummy is completed, a young author can read it to a partner or a group of classmates to see if the placement of the text works. This also helps the author get an idea of where pictures should be placed. In lengthier texts with limited illustration, students can still use this reading process to plan where to place pictures.

Once a young author is satisfied with the book's flow, the text can be transferred from the dummy copy to the formal book. Line guides—index stock with heavy black lines—can be positioned beneath each page to help authors write text evenly. Liquid correction fluid or white self-adhesive labels can camouflage any errors made on the final copy. If erasable crayons, such as Sanford® Plastic Markers, are used, changes in artwork can be made easily.

Words can be handwritten, typed, or printed with a computer. Depending on which of these processes is chosen, letters used can be a variety of styles and sizes. When writing text by hand, authors may enjoy experimenting with "shaky" writing for a spooky story, stylized ball letters for book covers, etc. Letters can also be shaped to resemble the word they represent. Certain word processing or printing programs allow writers to produce letters decked with bows or filled with stars and stripes! Some typewriters offer choices for changing the sizes and styles of letters, too.

CHOICES FOR ILLUSTRATIONS

Once the text has been written, the bookmaker is ready to add pictures. Sometimes, particularly with very young or less experienced authors, pictures may come first and be the inspiration for the text. Choosing to include special features like pages with lift-up flaps or peek-through holes adds another dimension to creating the artwork for the book.

Picture Sources

Children can select from many options when illustrating their books. The most popular and effective choice is usually their own original artwork. Drawing books, such as Ed Emberley's *Make a World: A Drawing Book,* give step-by-step instructions, which can help frustrated artists. Pictures cut from magazines, workbooks, calendars, coloring books, or travel or promotional brochures can be used for illustrations, as well as photographs, stickers, or postcards. Potato prints, commercial stamp sets, or stencils provide other sources for pictures. Additional illustration ideas using children's artwork are provided in section 2 (see SUMMER — Summer Fun).

Book Design

Pages of a book don't have to be rectangular. They can be cut into special shapes. For example, pages may be shaped like hearts (see FEBRUARY — Valentine's Day) or food items (see SUMMER — Summer Fun).

Another book design involves making a peek-through hole on each page that allows part of a picture on a subsequent page to be viewed. Through the hole, the reader might see a happy face, as in the *Days of the Week* book featured in SEPTEMBER — School Routines or a picture of themselves as described in NOVEMBER — Careers.

To add other interesting features to book illustrations, young authors can hide parts of pages with flaps, make portions of pictures pop out, or make wheels that turn. The Riddle section in the month of OCTOBER and the Animals section in the month of JANUARY include bookmaking ideas that employ flaps. Bookmakers can create flaps in two different ways by following these directions:

> Cut a piece of paper the desired size and shape of the flap. Fold back the top edge. Attach the edge of the flap to the book page with rubber cement or a glue stick.

or

> On a page of a blank book, cut three sides of a rectangle with a cutting blade. Fold the rectangle back to create a flap and a window opening in the page. Attach this page, but not the flap, with rubber cement or a glue stick to the page that follows it. Be careful not to get adhesive on the flap or it will not open. Words can be written or pictures mounted beneath the flap.

flap books   pop-up book   front-to-back and
                                                             back-to-front book

Young authors can use the same idea of attaching two adjacent pages together to create a book with rotating pictures. The flap can be removed from the window, and a wheel can be inserted between the two pages to show a picture through the window opening. As the wheel turns, different pictures can be seen through the window. Specific directions and applications are given in APRIL — Growing.

Joan Irvine's book *How to Make Pop-Ups* describes ideas for creating pop-ups. Specific instructions are given for measuring, folding, scoring, and cutting each project. Illustrated directions guide students through each step of the process.

Books can be designed to be read from front to back, then flipped upside down to be read from back to front. This format can be used to make a book containing two short stories, as described in OCTOBER — Halloween, or one story that starts and ends with the same event, like the life cycle book in APRIL — Growing.

Books can be created using envelopes that are stitched or stapled together. Letters or other messages can then be tucked into the envelopes. Instructions and examples of envelope books using a blank book are presented in FEBRUARY — Valentine's Day.

CHANCES FOR COMPUTER USE

Young authors can use the computer to simplify the procedures of revising text, personalizing stories, creating graphics, and producing a polished final product. The following section gives ideas for using the computer at various stages of the bookmaking process — writing drafts, revising text, creating graphics, and publishing final copy.

Word Processing

A teacher, a parent, or a child can use word processing software to personalize text, to create and finish "story starters," or to write original stories. Young authors with some computer experience can use the word processor to write their own stories on computer, while those with less experience can dictate stories to someone at the keyboard. An advantage to using the computer is that typing mistakes are easily corrected by retyping letters or words. Also, the revision process is less painful, because text can be altered or moved with a keystroke.

In addition to standard word processing features, certain word processors allow the choice of different fonts (type styles), changes in the sizes of letters, or use of a rebus alphabet. In a rebus alphabet, typing *R* might produce a rabbit symbol, and typing *r* could create a picture of a ring. If a word processing package that incorporates a rebus alphabet is used, older children could write stories in a picture code for friends to decipher, or pictures could be substituted for some of the words in a story dictated by a younger child.

Personalizing text becomes fast and easy when using a word processor. Words of traditional songs, poems, or nursery rhymes or young authors' own variations can be typed into the computer using word processing software. The "Find and Replace" feature can be used to change characters' names to the names of young authors.

For holidays, unit topics, or special occasions, you may want to make "sentence starters." See the NOVEMBER computer idea for an example that features a special family member. This method can help keep children focused on the topic, as well as giving a class book a more predictable text.

Graphics

Pictures to accompany the text can be made on the computer using a graphics program and can be printed with a dot matrix printer. Some software allows use of the keyboard for input. Other programs use input devices, such as a joystick, a mouse, a Koala Pad™, or another graphics tablet. When teachers or parents are purchasing graphics software, they should check that the software chosen will work with the computers and printers they are using. The graphics program they select should be easy for children to use, have some basic shapes built in, and allow placement of text on the picture. Other useful features include "cloning" (making additional copies of your picture on the same screen), rotating (printing your picture sideways), enlarging, and reducing. See the JANUARY computer ideas for additional details.

Integrated Programs

Because text is not as easy to manipulate in graphics programs as it is in word processing programs, for longer stories young authors may want to alternate pages of text written with the word processor with graphics printouts. Some software programs, such as *SuperPrint!*™, *The Print Shop*™, and *Printmaster Plus*™, allow integration of text and graphics, and include some pre-made pictures. While these packages don't provide as many features as most drawing programs or word processors, they do simplify mixing words and pictures for bookmaking. These programs offer add-on disk libraries with many choices of letter styles — letters surrounded by hearts or ribbons, letters with bells, etc. These programs can be used to create a border for a book page, leaving the middle of the page blank. Put the same page through the computer a second time and print a story on it using the word processor.

Publishing

When books are written using the computer, multiple copies can be printed at the touch of a key, making it easy for young authors to share their work with each other. Stories written on the computer can be printed out on self-adhesive computer labels that stick easily in hardbound blank books. When graphics are being included, authors might choose to mount the full printout in a blank book, or to assemble pages using one of the other bindings described later in this chapter. The MAY computer idea provides additional pointers on how to use desktop publishing for distribution of students' work.

Section 2 of this book offers monthly ideas for making books with the computer. These suggestions will appear in a box with a special symbol.

CHOICES FOR BOOK ASSEMBLY

Before assembling their books, young authors need to consider where they will place certain components. They may want to include a title page and a dedication page at the beginning of the book. The last page can be reserved for readers to write their reactions to the book and compliments to the author. Depending on the purpose of the book, other features may be selected, such as a table of contents, an index, or a glossary.

There are a variety of ways the pieces of a book may be put together. Young authors can assemble their text and illustrations using hardbound blank books, cardboard books, photo albums, accordian books, or loose-leaf notebooks.

Blank Books

Hardbound blank books provide a pleasing finished appearance. Because of the pride young authors feel in seeing their own completed hardbound books, teachers should strive to make it possible for each child in their classrooms to make a hardbound book at least once every school year. In addition, teachers will want to plan to make one or two class books each month in hardbound versions that can be added to the classroom or school library.

Permanent markers work well for decorating the covers of hardbound blank books. Watercolor markers can also be used on the covers if an acrylic spray, such as Krylon® by Borden®, or clear self-adhesive plastic, such as ConTac® paper, is used to prevent smearing. Watercolor markers, crayons, colored pencils, or ballpoint pens may be used on the inside pages of a book. Young authors should not use permanent markers inside their books unless they plan to use only one side of each page, because the marker ink will penetrate the paper. When using watercolor markers inside the book, it is helpful to place plain pieces of paper between the pages until the ink from the markers dries. This prevents wet ink on one page from transferring to the facing page. Also, paper can be put between the pages when working with crayons, as crayon tends to smear from one page to the next while the opposite side of the page is being colored.

To mount photos or other pictures in blank books, children can use rubber cement, a glue stick, or double-stick tape. Liquid white glue contains too much moisture. It may wrinkle or discolor both the book pages and the illustrations. Young authors can follow these instructions to get a very strong bond using rubber cement:

1. Draw lightly around the picture on the book page.
2. Brush rubber cement inside the marked area and on the back of the picture to be mounted.
3. Let both surfaces dry to touch before placing the picture in the book.

If preferred, rubber cement can be applied just to the back of the picture and not to the book page. This process is faster, but the edges of the picture tend to pull up after long use. For more durability, adding clear self-adhesive plastic will protect the pages, as well as help secure the pictures. Rubber cement or a glue stick can also be used to mount clear adhesive pockets from photo albums on the pages of a blank book to hold photos. Then photographs can be changed as desired.

Other Binding Choices

While there is seldom a more satisfying binding than the hardbound blank books provide, at times teachers or parents may wish to offer some alternative binding styles. For a young child, a cardboard-weight book is sometimes desirable. Teachers or parents can watch for clearance sales on "board" books for toddlers. Pages of the book can be covered with a plain color of self-adhesive plastic, and a permanent marker can be used to write and draw on the newly created pages. As an alternative, text and pictures can be created on plain white paper cut to the size of the book pages. Rubber cement can be used to fasten the paper to the book's cardboard pages. Then the book can be covered with clear self-adhesive plastic.

For a different style of cardboard book, posterboard pages can be cut in any sizes and shapes desired. After text is written and pictures are drawn, the pages can be laminated or covered with clear self-adhesive plastic. Plastic teeth binding can be used to bind pages together. If a binding machine is not available to teachers at their school or district resource center, the book can be taken to a print shop that offers that service. Fees are usually modest. Another possibility is to punch holes in the cardboard pages and tie them together with yarn, or secure with metal notebook rings or colorful Chinese jacks.

Photo albums of all sorts can be used for bookmaking. Large ones with self-adhesive pages, small ones with slide-in pockets, and notebook-style loose-leaf albums are just a few of the many available choices. Plastic sheet protectors can be used to hold book pages in a three-ring binder.

A small accordian book can be made by using stiff adding machine paper and folding it like a paper fan. Cardboard covers can be added to the front and back if desired. An accordian book with larger pages can be created using shelf paper. Paper can be stitched or stapled together to produce books. For instance, to create a twenty-eight page 5½" x 8" book, fold seven 8½" x 11" sheets of paper in half. Sew along the fold line, or staple with a long-reach stapler. These are great for rough drafts before using a hardbound blank book for a final edition.

Bookmaking gives young authors many choices when selecting the right materials for making their books. The number of choices and chances available help ensure that each book made will reflect the unique personality of its author.

Chapter 4

Developing the Desire to Read and Write

In children's daily instruction, the focus is often on the mechanics of reading and writing. If children who know how to read and write never pick up a book or a pencil in their leisure time, how successful was the instruction? Although teaching the mechanics of literacy is important, encouraging the love of reading and writing is even more essential. In this chapter, we present ideas to help encourage all children to read for pleasure, write for enjoyment, and celebrate authorship.

ENCOURAGING READING

Reading and writing are interrelated. An interesting idea encountered while reading a book may spark a young author to create a new story. After the story is written, classmates will be encouraged to read it. Once the story has been read, listeners may be inspired to try out a writing idea of their own, and the cycle continues. If students are going to be encouraged to write, they need to be encouraged to read as well. To promote reading as an enjoyable activity, parents and teachers can provide children with time to read for pleasure, inviting materials for leisure reading, and creative ways to promote books.

Time to Read

Teachers and parents should strive to provide time for children to read for pleasure. One method of doing this is to provide ten to fifteen minutes of D.E.A.R. (Drop Everything and Read) time daily. Students spend this time reading enjoyable books even if school assignments or household chores are not yet completed. This is not a time for the teacher to grade papers or parents to do the dishes — the adults read for pleasure during this time, too! In some schools, the entire building gets involved by setting aside twenty-five minutes once or twice a week where *everyone*, including the principal and secretaries, reads a book of his or her choice. In the home, time for silent reading can be reserved after dinner or before bedtime. D.E.A.R. time also gives children and parents a chance to read aloud their favorite books, stories, or poems.

Materials to Read

The home or classroom library should be well stocked with children's books and magazines available for D.E.A.R. or other leisure reading time. These books may be written by students and teachers, borrowed from the school or public library, and purchased at garage sales and used book sales. Public libraries often sell books discarded from their collections at very reasonable rates.

Magazine subscriptions offer new issues that can be used for current reading materials, while older issues may be taken apart to use in illustrating stories or making books. Magazines available for children include *Chick-A-Dee, Owl, Sesame Street, Ranger Rick, Your Big Backyard, Highlights,* and *National Geographic World.* (See the bibliography for additional information.) Old issues can often be purchased quite inexpensively at used book sales. These magazines may contain series of articles that can be combined to create a book. Children, parents, or teachers can simply slide the pages into plastic page protectors and assemble in a three-ring binder.

Promoting Books

Teachers and parents can plan activities to promote reading. Instead of assigning standard book reports, teachers can encourage students to design posters, create bookmarks, or videotape commercials advertising books they've read. One student's recommendation can really motivate another child to read a book. Other activities to promote reading books include:

- a brief puppet show
- dramatization of a scene for the class
- a diorama (three-dimensional scene inside a shoe box)
- oral book reviews, similar to movie reviews seen on TV

ENCOURAGING WRITING

Children should be given many opportunities to experience writing as a joyful activity. Parents and teachers can help by offering time for writing, a wide variety of materials for writing and bookmaking, and a place to send and receive written messages.

Time for Writing

Students should have time available for writing daily. How can teachers find time in the busy day for students to write? As students arrive in the classroom and wait for the school day to begin, they can work on their journals. In these journals, children can freely collect ideas and shape stories, just as they might doodle and sketch illustrations. By rehearsing their writing and drawing in the journals, students are ready to refine and edit their ideas in second and third drafts for possible bookmaking.

Teachers may allow journal writing to replace some of the work sheets or workbook pages that might normally be used during the morning. After lunch and recess, students can write in their journals while classmates use the rest rooms and get drinks of water. Teachers should be careful that time is scheduled for journal writing and that it is not left as a filler activity for the end of a lesson or the end of a day, because there will rarely be that extra time for the writing (see MAY — Journals).

As an enrichment activity, an after-school bookmaking club provides students with additional opportunities for writing. A teacher or a parent acts as a sponsor to help supervise the students, and plan the weekly or monthly activities. The group may be called the B.E.A.R. C.U.B.s (Be Enthusiastic About Reading — Create Unique Books), and teddy bear buttons can be made for each child in the group. Bookplates can be added to books made by club members for themselves or as gifts for others (see Appendix).

At home, parents can also encourage children to take time for writing. Letters, thank-you notes, shopping lists, and diaries provide natural writing opportunities for children. When siblings squabble, parents can redirect hostile feelings by asking children to write about how they feel and describe what happened. Families can set aside time once a month to create a book together based on family experiences (see monthly ideas in section 2).

Writing Center

Young authors should have easy access to writing and bookmaking materials, and special times available to use those materials. Teachers can create writing centers in their classrooms, where children can go to create stories and books. A center can be as simple as an extra desk stocked with "story starter" idea cards, interesting paper, and a variety of markers, pencils, and pens, or as complex as a multiactivity learning center, with several kinds of writing and bookmaking activities going on simultaneously.

Reference books, such as different types of dictionaries, a thesaurus, and a writing style manual, can be housed at the writing center to help young authors as they plan and create stories. Two helpful books that explain the writing process from rough draft to published book are *How a Book Is Made* by Aliki and *I Can Be an Author* by Ray Broekel. Additional items that might be included in the writing center are:

- wordless cartoon strips
- photos of class activities
- old magazines and catalogs
- tape and a stapler
- a typewriter or a computer with a printer

Postcards, envelopes, and sticker "stamps" from junk mail advertisements can be used to inspire letter writing. The teacher should have a supply of postage stamps as well, for times when that well-written letter should really be sent! School and public librarians can help children locate addresses of authors, sports heroes, or other celebrities.

A writing center can be set up in the home by gathering the materials mentioned previously and placing them in a special cabinet, drawer, or desk where they are readily available for children. Easy access to reference books should be provided as well.

Bookmaking Supplies

In addition to writing supplies, materials for bookmaking should be readily available to students. Items such as a stapler, a paper punch, and yarn could be included in the classroom writing center. Other supplies might be placed on a cart in the school media center, which could be wheeled to classrooms as needed. A bookmaking cart for the school might include:

- hardbound blank books in a variety of covers
- a long-reach stapler
- a plastic-teeth binding machine
- cardboard and paper cut to desired page sizes
- a three-hole paper punch
- yarn, needles, and thread
- old magazines to cut up for illustrations
- resource books containing creative writing and bookmaking ideas

A parent group might be willing to provide volunteer help and funds needed to purchase the supplies.

Some schools purchase hardbound blank books in quantity and sell them to students in the school bookstore. This encourages children to buy books to make at home, as well as at school. Other bookmaking supplies, such as markers, clear plastic adhesive, and photo albums, could be made available as well. Brochures can be sent home to parents several times a year describing blank hardbound books and their uses. Bulk orders can then be placed.

CELEBRATING AUTHORSHIP

In many ways, bookmaking is its own reward. Young authors experience increasing pride as they shape their words and pictures. They watch the buds of their ideas grow into the sturdy plants of rough drafts, and see intermediate drafts blossom into finished books. All authors, young and old, feel the need to share their completed work with others. An opportunity to receive recognition and to celebrate authorship in a variety of ways can be offered to young authors in the home, in the community, and in the school.

In the Home

A home celebration can honor a book made at home or at school. The book may be one created by a single author in the family, or it could be one collaborated on by two or more family members. A special dinner could be part of the event, perhaps with a cake decorated as a book for dessert.

Special guests, such as family friends or relatives, could be invited to attend the celebration. After dinner, family members can read aloud the books they have made. For additional impact, these readings could be recorded with a tape recorder or video camera, and the recordings saved as a family keepsake. Copies of the tape could be sent to relatives in other towns or taken to school to share with classmates.

In the Community

Local television or radio talk shows can be contacted to see if they might be willing to interview a few of a school's young authors. The public library could reserve a special section for circulating books authored by schoolchildren. An enterprising classroom could arrange to publish an anthology of their writing to sell in the school or at local bookstores (see MAY — Journals).

Communities might plan a weekend event at a local mall or library to honor young authors. Books created by young authors could be put on display in a prominent place in the community, such as a bank lobby, a glass case in a restaurant, a store, or a booth at a county fair.

In the School

Children will feel their books are appreciated if class time is provided for them to read their books aloud. The teacher can recognize students' book-making efforts with inexpensive awards, such as reproducible certificates or bookmarks (see appendix for reproducible samples). A pizza party at lunch-time or light refreshments in the early afternoon could accompany the festivities.

Young authors can receive support for their work through the school and the community, as well as from their families, classmates, and teachers. Parent-teacher organizations or local businesses may be willing to help underwrite school bookmaking celebrations. A school cafeteria or a caterer might be willing to donate services or refreshments.

Excerpts from books students have written could be published in the school or community newspaper. A press release with photographs could also be prepared and submitted for possible publication. Children should be encouraged to submit texts from their books to magazines that publish children's work. Original picture books created by children can be submit-ted to the book writing competition sponsored by School Book Fair. Each year, a winning book is published. (See appendix for titles and addresses.)

A school celebration could take the form of an early morning breakfast, a special lunch menu, an afternoon tea, or an evening open house. Authors and their families might vote for their favorite books in a variety of categories. A limousine rental service could be asked to offer a free ride home from school to the author who receives the most votes for his or her book. Family bookmaking might be recognized during the event as well, by encouraging families to share and display books made at home.

A professional author or illustrator might be featured as a speaker, with book readings by selected young authors scheduled as part of the celebra-tion. In small groups, students could share their books with peers and fami-ly members. The young authors' books could also be arranged on tables thematically or by grade level for others to read, with samples of illustra-tions displayed on the walls. If the final page of each book is left blank, readers might add their comments to the author.

Special bookplates (see B.E.A.R. C.U.B. bookplate in appendix) could be attached to the inside covers of the books. Embossed gold seals might be placed on the outside covers to make every child's creation look like a ''real'' award winner. Finally, each young author would receive a recogni-tion certificate or a ribbon for their participation. For help in planning a Young Author's Celebration, consult the checklist in the appendix.

Parents and teachers can help young authors develop a desire to read and write by providing interesting materials and inviting experiences. When allowed time to choose from a variety of enjoyable reading and writing ac-tivities, students discover that reading and writing are fun!

Chapter 5

Energetic, Enthusiastic Examples

Enthusiasm for bookmaking becomes contagious when people see how worthwhile and special the experience is. Through bookmaking, teachers and parents can provide experiences that integrate reading and writing for children. In books, they can record memories and supply additional background information for children. Bookmaking also provides the opportunity for children to become engaged in an activity that is purposeful and meaningful. The books created by children become unique records of their language development and personal experiences.

To get people excited about bookmaking takes energetic, enthusiastic teachers, parents, and children, all involved in authorship.

TEACHERS AND PARENTS

Both teachers and parents can be energetic, enthusiastic examples to young authors. When they read books aloud and participate in silent reading experiences with children, they demonstrate the joy of book reading. As they create books for and with children, they send the message that bookmaking is indeed a valuable activity worth the time and effort they put into it.

Not only do children benefit from books read or created, but they also become increasingly aware of the writing and reading processes. They witness adults stumble and correct themselves when reading a story aloud. They see adults crumple up first drafts, use dictionaries to locate word spellings, and mutter to themselves as they reread what they have written. These demonstrations are necessary to nurture literacy.

Teachers and parents can be examples for one another as well. A teacher who is excited about a great book read or a special classroom bookmaking project can share ideas with parents through the class newsletter. Teachers can run bookmaking workshops to help parents with ideas for family books. In school workrooms or at professional meetings, teachers can trade bookmaking ideas and show samples of books they or the children have created.

Parents, as well as grandparents, can support teachers by helping with bookmaking activities in the home and serving as volunteers in the classroom. Families can make books that can be shared with the children's classes at school or with friends at home. When showing off a family-made book, parents can encourage other families to create their own editions for home libraries.

YOUNG AUTHORS

Young authors excite other children about reading and writing. At school, videotaped interviews of young authors and displays of their writing drafts can be made to demonstrate each stage of bookmaking. As children see the videos of their peers engaged in creating books, they may discover a new writing strategy or a different design technique, or be inspired to make books of their own.

Children also set an example of authorship by reading their own books to their classmates, to other students in their school, or to their siblings at home. In the children's section of the library or at a conference for young authors, child-made books may be featured for others to read and enjoy. Young authors can influence their parents and teachers by the enthusiasm they display and the clever ideas they use when making books. This often encourages adults to plan more bookmaking activities.

The excitement generated by parents, teachers, and children as authors sets an example to others and invites them to try bookmaking — it's an effort worth taking!

Section

2

Ideas to Inspire Young Authors

This second section presents a variety of ideas and specific directions organized under themes for each month:

SEPTEMBER — School Routines, Classmates and Field Trips
OCTOBER — Fall, Halloween, and Riddles
NOVEMBER — Family, Friends, and Careers
DECEMBER — Gifts, Traditions, and Holidays
JANUARY — Animals, Habitats, and Winter
FEBRUARY — Valentine's Day, Presidents' Day, and Dental Health
  Month
MARCH — Past, Present, and Future
APRIL — Spring, Weather, and Growing
MAY — Histories, Yearbooks, and Journals
SUMMER — ''Reading Rainbow,'' Summer Fun, and Potpourri

We hope that you, whether parent or teacher, will become inspired to make books for and with children throughout the year.

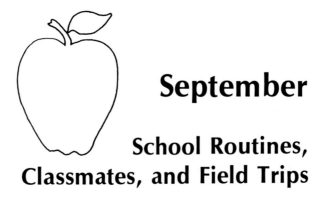

September

School Routines, Classmates, and Field Trips

When school opens in the fall, students face new teachers, routines, and classmates. To ease the children's transition, teachers and parents can help them create books about their new experiences in school and on field trips planned during the month of September. Try one of these suggested bookmaking activities with your children.

SCHOOL ROUTINES

One way to help children through the first days or weeks is to design a book that describes a school's routine. This book can be written by narrating the day's activities. A teacher or a parent can make the book or enlist the children to help. Each child could supply a description of one of the day's activities, accompanied by a drawing or selected magazine pictures for illustrations. Photographs taken of the students throughout the day could also be used.

Another pattern for a routine book is offered in Sesyle Joslin's books, *What Do You Say, Dear?* and *What Do You Do, Dear?* She describes different situations and asks what you should say or do. To write a book using this style, you might ask the children to think of questions about classroom daily procedures, such as:

What do you do, dear, when you arrive at school?
    Put my book bag on my hook.
What do you do, dear, when school starts?
    Get in my seat and be quiet.
What do you say, dear, when the teacher calls your name?
    Present.

Each child can contribute an idea for a page by making up a question and giving the appropriate response or rule for a variety of school situations, for example, when the tornado siren blows or when a meal is served.

You can also create a manners or classroom conduct book with the children to serve as a reminder of the way you want them to talk and act. Joe Scruggs's song "Abracadabra," on his album by the same name, tells a story about a boy who forgets the "magic words" of *please* and *thank you*. This imaginative song offers a springboard for children to invent stories about when they forgot the polite words to use.

For most of us working with preschoolers or elementary-grade students, September means getting back to a weekly routine. Each day of the week may have something particular that the children should keep in mind, for instance,

Monday is gym class — remember to wear sneakers.
Tuesday is library time — remember to return books.
Wednesday is...

Even for the very young child not yet in school, each day of the week brings activities that have some degree of predictability:

Monday — laundry day
Tuesday — shopping day
Wednesday...

Teachers and parents can utilize this theme with bookmaking to help each child understand the week's schedule.

To create a weekly routine book, you may want to use the following predictable text, substituting what you do each day:

Monday, I'm happy to *go to the grocery story.*
Tuesday, I'm happy to *go to art class.*
Wednesday, I'm happy to _____

Continue this pattern for each day of the week, then end as follows:

Monday, Tuesday, Wednesday, Thursday, Friday, Saturday,
Sunday — these are the happy days of my week!

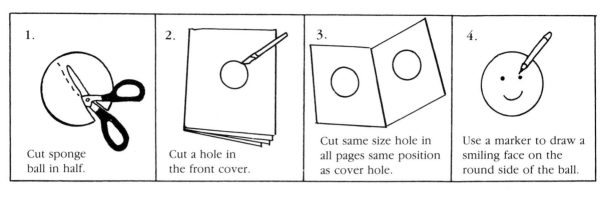

1. Cut sponge ball in half.

2. Cut a hole in the front cover.

3. Cut same size hole in all pages same position as cover hole.

4. Use a marker to draw a smiling face on the round side of the ball.

5. Glue flat side of the ball to inside back cover.

6. Rubber cement pages together in pairs to create a seven-page book.

7. Write text on front side of each page.

You can illustrate the book with happy-face stickers or children's drawings. To be more elaborate, cut a sponge ball in half, then use a knife to cut a round hole out of the cover and each page of a blank book. Draw a smile and eyes on the half sponge ball, and mount the ball on the inside back cover so that it fits through the circles cut out of the front cover and pages. With rubber cement, glue the pages together in pairs to create a seven-page book. On the front side of each page, write the text to describe how each day makes the child(ren) happy. This idea can easily be adapted for a book about activities in different months and for special holidays during the year.

Teachers and parents can ask children to describe their school or personal schedules through the use of the alphabet as a pattern for a book's text. Using each letter, assist the children to associate objects or activities with the correct letter:

A is for *a*fternoon when we all get together for kindergarten.
B is for the fifteen *b*oys in the class...

You can challenge the students by modifying the alphabet pattern, as Mary Elting and Michael Folsom do in their book *Q Is for Duck*. Instead of the obvious letter-item association, the pairings are much more obscure, for instance,

C is for school. Do you know why?
Because my school's name is Collegewood.
D is for water fountain. Do you know why?
Because you can get a drink there.

CLASSMATES

Another bookmaking idea that helps students work together is to create a book about the members of a class. To start, you can ask the children to write about themselves, or, in pairs, to interview each other for short biographical sketches. Be sure to include a contribution about yourself as well as other personnel involved with the students, such as specialized teachers, librarians, assistants, volunteers, the nurse, the principal, secretaries, custodians, and others. This book will be one of the most popular books in your classroom.

Books about school routines and classmates can be shared throughout the year with visiting parents, student teachers, or new students to help them learn about your classroom and your expectations. Parents and children can

Autobiographies

Computer Idea

To assist in the creation of a class book, you may want to use the computer.

At the beginning of the school year, have each person in your classroom (including yourself) complete a story starter to get to know each other better. For children who already have some competence in using the computer, give group instruction on how to delete each blank and enter their own words (see your word processing manual for details). The story reads

My name is _____. When I am home, two of my favorite things to do are _____ and _____.
I have (or wish for) a pet_____named_____.
I go to _____school. My favorite activity at school is_____because _____.
I am in _____class.
Something I hope to do in our class this year is _____.

As the students fill in the blanks, you may want to encourage them to add sentences to the original story or delete lines that don't pertain to them. When done, create a page border using a printing program, and make enough copies for the class. Use a large type style to print each child's name at the top of the story he or she wrote. To illustrate the book, take a snapshot of each child or ask them to bring pictures from home.

Alternatively, students can draw self-portraits, or they can be paired with a partner to draw each other. Attach the computer printouts to the pages of a blank book using a glue stick, or punch holes to place the pages in a three-ring binder.

make books to remember what a particular age and grade was like. In addition, special books can record class or home activities during the year. These books can be organized weekly, monthly, seasonally, or by special events, such as trips or holidays.

FIELD TRIPS

A field trip is a perfect bookmaking opportunity. Most teachers invite children to retell their experiences on a field trip in a language experience story. Written on chart paper or the blackboard, such a story might read like this:

> Today we went to the apple orchard.
> We rode on the school bus and two mothers came along.
> We saw the trees with apples and we each got to pick one and eat it.
> We went to see where they sell the apples. We saw them making apple cider there, too.
> We bought some cider to bring back to class to drink.

A language experience story is wonderful for children's participation because they love to see their ideas put in print. The language experience story also serves as a first draft for children to edit and polish into a final draft for a field trip book.

After completing a language experience story, teachers can request a committee of students to rewrite the text for a book. If the story was written on chart paper, the children can cut apart the sentences and then reword or resequence the information. Once the revisions are made, the assigned students can ask for class approval and then write their text in a blank book. Brochures, maps, postcards, magazine pictures, photographs, or children's drawings about the trip can illustrate the book. Parents can follow the same procedure by asking their child to retell an experience and assisting with revisions to create a book.

The field trip book can be made more exciting by using one of the following writing patterns based on books. In *The Day Jimmy's Boa Ate the Wash*, Trinka Hakes Noble describes a class field trip to a farm backward, through

54

questions and answers. The field trip to the apple orchard described previously could appear as follows:

> How was your field trip?
>   It was fine until Mary ate a worm.
> What? Mary ate a worm?
>   Yes, she didn't see the worm in the apple because she
>   was trying not to step in the spilt cider.
> How did the cider spill?

Dr. Seuss offers another descriptive style that encourages imagination in his book *And to Think That I Saw It on Mulberry Street*. The young boy in his story tries to create a more exciting account of what he saw on his walk home from school. Although this book can serve as a model for children expanding on their common trip home from school daily, it can also stimulate creative thoughts about a field trip. Instead of describing the ride in the bus to an apple orchard, the children might say:

> We flew in a large helicopter to the apple orchard while some of the class arrived in hot air balloons. The trees were covered with apples of enormous sizes, which were almost as big as the students. We had to help each other to pick an apple...

Another book design that can serve as a catalyst for students' writing is supplied by Joanna Cole in the series of "Magic School Bus" adventures in which students describe their field trips. Besides telling what children did during an outing, Cole includes students' reports on a topic. Teachers can ask students to research information that might accompany a field trip book. For example, for the trip to the apple orchard, students could investigate the different types of apples or the procedure for making cider.

Making books on trips, school, or classmates helps children remember their experiences and compare them from year to year.

October

Fall, Halloween, and Riddles

October is an exciting month for children. Enthusiasm builds as preparations for Halloween and plans for costumes are made. Parents, teachers, and students can take this opportunity to create books of poems, songs, riddles, and stories about fall and Halloween.

FALL

Fall leaves make an interesting topic for a matching game book. First, cut the pages of a large blank book in half horizontally. Children can then mount a picture of a different leaf on the top half of the front side of each page. Alternatively, crayon rubbings of the leaves or real leaves covered with clear contact paper could be used. Names and descriptions of the various kinds of trees the leaves came from can be written on the bottom halves of the front sides of the pages at random. Once the book is assembled, students match the leaf on the top half of a page to its name and description on the bottom half of a page. When the corresponding pages are found, readers look at the back side of the pages, which have been marked with matching shapes or other symbols to allow self-checking of answers.

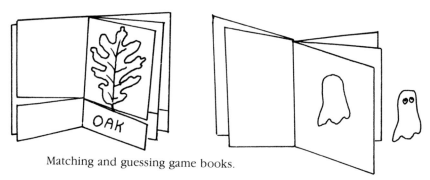

Matching and guessing game books.

Autumn leaves burning may create smoke that children imagine to be many different shapes. Share with them the story of eerie lights appearing over bogs and marshes that fired the imaginations of English residents during fall seasons in the 1900s. Some names given to the lights were Lantern Men, Hob-'O-Lantern, and Will-O'-the-Wisp. People believed that if they followed these characters, they would be led into a swamp to die. Scientists later discovered the true reason for the strange lights. See Edna Barth's book *Witches, Pumpkins, and Grinning Ghosts* for more details about the legend.

Brainstorm other situations in which people have seen objects that appear to be different than they really are. Record the ideas on the blackboard or on chart paper. Ask the children to draw a picture that could appear to be something other than what it really is, with a caption written underneath. These drawings can first be used as an October bulletin board display, then later pasted into a blank book for use in the class library.

Share with the class two books by Child's Play, *A Book of Ghosts* and *I thought I saw,* which feature cutouts in each page showing what the author thought he saw. When the page is turned, the reader sees a full picture that reveals something quite different than what was seen through the hole in the previous page.

For a bookmaking challenge, have each child draw a page of clouds, smoke, tree branches, or another background that could easily be seen as something other than what it actually represents. Then have each one cut the shape of what else that picture might look like from a piece of tagboard. Use this template and a matte knife to cut a hole in the page of a blank book, being sure to place a piece of cardboard behind the page being cut. The child's drawing is positioned and mounted on the next page. Students can create rhyming text or descriptive prose to accompany their pictures.

HALLOWEEN

At Halloween, even children appear to be something different than themselves! Because dressing up is an important part of Halloween festivities, children may enjoy reading or listening to books about different costumes, and then creating books of their own with that theme. Robert Bright's *Georgie's Halloween* features the ghost Georgie, who goes to a party where a prize will be given for the best Halloween costume. In *The Humbug Witch* by Lorna Balian, a witch puts on her clothing piece by piece.

After reading or listening to these stories, children can use the following poem to make books recalling their personal experiences and memories of dressing up at Halloween time.

I wore a _____ costume when I was one,
and thought Halloween was lots of fun.

I dressed like a _____ when I was two,
and was a little bit scared when the ghosts said, BOO!

A _____ is what I pretended to be
on the Halloween when I was three.

I was disguised as a _____ when I was four,
and said "Trick-or-Treat" at the neighbor's door.

When I was five years old on Halloween,
I was the (prettiest, scariest, etc.) _____
you've ever seen.

On Halloween when I was six,
I was a _____ to do my tricks.

Then I was seven, and know how I dressed?
I was a _____, and nobody guessed!

On Halloween when I was eight,
my_____ costume was really great.

Continue the pattern through the child's current age, and end with:

Each Halloween, I've loved my disguise, and giving my friends a surprise!

Parents could get involved in this bookmaking project by supplying photos and helping children remember how they dressed each year.

Songs can provide more Halloween bookmaking ideas. Listen to Hap Palmer's song "Witches' Brew" (on the album of the same name), which describes a variety of "icky" things a witch puts into her brew. Use the instrumental version of the song to let children make up their own ingredients for the brew. Afterward, children can each write their own recipes for a witch's cookbook. For more ideas, they can take a look at Marjorie Winslow's *Mud Pies and Other Recipes,* which features such delicacies as "Roast Rocks" and "Pencil Sharpener Pudding."

The song "Five Little Pumpkins" is a favorite one this time of year. To recreate the song in story form, students each put a gate with a fence on the front sides of the first eight sheets of a blank book. The gate and fence can be drawn with markers or crayon, or cut from construction paper and pasted into the book. Children use an orange stamp pad or marker to color their thumbs and stamp five thumbprints above each of the first seven gates. The eighth gate remains empty. Then they draw a jack-o'-lantern face on each thumbprint.

The students fill in the following text, or an original variation, on each page. The words in quotations can be placed in cartoon bubbles over the speaking pumpkins.

1. Five little pumpkins sitting on a gate.
2. The first one said, "Oh my, it's getting late."
3. The second one said, "There are witches in the air."
4. The third one said, "But we don't care!"
5. The fourth one said, "Let's run and run and run!"
6. The fifth one said, "I'm ready for some fun."
7. Ooo-oo went the wind and out went the light.
8. And the five little pumpkins rolled out of sight.

The front covers can be decorated with a gate, jack-o'-lantern thumbprints, and the book's title. At this point, one cover and eight of a book's fourteen pages have been used.

Flip a book upside down, and turn it so that the blank back cover opens as a front cover would. Another Halloween book can be made using this as its cover and the next six blank sheets for text and illustrations. You could use the following "Five Little Ghosts" computer idea for these empty pages.

If you prefer not to use a computer, the ghost idea is still applicable for the extra pages of "Five Little Pumpkins" by writing in the text with a marker or colored pencil instead.

Five Little Ghosts

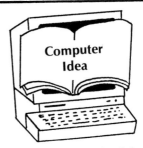

Computer Idea

Children can use word processing software to create a ghost book based on the traditional counting song "The Elephant Song." If you're not familiar with the tune, listen to Sharon, Lois, and Bram's rendition of it on their album, *Elephant Show Record*. At Halloween, an adaptation of the song could be

One little ghost went out to play
In a haunted house one day.
He had such frightening fun
That he called for another little ghost to come,
"HEY, GHOST!"

Two little ghosts went out to play
In a haunted house one day.
They had such frightening fun
That they called for another little ghost to come,
"HEY, GHOST!"

Continue the pattern through five ghosts, then end with:

Five little ghosts went out to play
All in a haunted house one day.
And when it came to be Halloween night,
They left the house to give everyone a fright!

BOO!

Children can use this version or create their own variation of the song, with the additional challenge of substituting new nouns and verbs, such as

One little witch went out to fly,
On her broom in the sky.

Using the computer, young authors can quickly create multiple verses of the song. After typing one verse, they can reproduce that verse with just a few keystrokes, using the "copy" feature of the word processor. Minor text changes needed for each new verse can easily be made. Pictures and songs can follow the original text, or variations can be tried. Children can draw and color illustrations, or create them from Halloween stickers and wall decorations.

As another option, you could ask your students to generate some Halloween nursery rhymes to finish the book, for instance,

> Old Mr. Skeleton sat on a wall,
> Old Mr. Skeleton had a great fall.
> And all (school's name) girls,
> And all (school's name) boys,
> Covered their ears and ran from the noise.

For other inspiration on creating Halloween nursery rhymes, listen to Scholastic's record *Mother Ghost Nursery Rhymes* by Joseph Rapaso.

RIDDLES

To further inspire your students' creativity, show them Eric Hill's *Nursery Rhyme PEEK-A-BOOK*, which hides the answers to nursery rhyme riddles behind flaps. Then read the book *The Twisted Witch and Other Spooky Riddles* by David Adler, and let students make up their own Halloween riddles. Using shaky (scary) writing, riddles can be written in flaps of construction paper that will be pasted into a blank book. Answers to the riddles should be written on the book pages underneath the flaps. Children's original artwork can be used to illustrate. Supplement with Halloween stickers or stamps if desired.

Another riddle book with flaps can be made featuring students in Halloween costumes. To help your students create this class book, ask them to follow these steps:

1. Draw and color a picture of yourself in a Halloween costume.
   Cut out the picture with an extra tab on the left side. Fold the tab so that it goes underneath the costume.
2. Using a glue stick, attach the back of the tab to a page in a blank book. The costume has now become a flap.
3. On the part of the page beneath the flap, draw a picture of yourself in regular clothing.

Each student will use one page for his or her costume and picture.

| 1. Draw self in a costume. Cut out with space for a tab at the left. | 2. Fold tab and glue to the page. The drawing is now a flap. | 3. Draw self in regular clothes under the flap. Use one page for each student. |

The text could read, "Who is this?" The child's name could be printed under the costume flap. Children will delight in guessing which of their friends is under each disguise. Parents using this idea with children at home may want to include photos of the children and their friends behind the costume flaps in place of drawings.

Your class will enjoy the game in Marcia and Michael Folsom's *Easy as Pie,* which organizes riddles about familiar sayings alphabetically. Children can compose an original alphabet book of Halloween similes following this pattern. The first four pages might read:

> PAGE ONE: *A* Red as a poison
> PAGE TWO: Apple
> PAGE THREE: *B* Evil as a witch's
> PAGE FOUR: Bat.

Continue in this style for each letter of the alphabet. This pattern can easily be used for riddle books on other subjects as well.

As October ends, the new books in your classroom library that feature ideas about fall, Halloween, and riddles will be read eagerly by the young authors who helped create them.

November

Family, Friends, and Careers

November is the time of year when we reflect on being thankful, and this provides a theme for a variety of books that can be written about family members and friends. It can also be a time for children to think about what they would like to be when they grow up. Teachers and parents can help children create special books using this month's ideas.

FAMILY

As an intitiating activity, teachers may like to use a song to help students consider for whom they are thankful. Hap Palmer's song "Things I'm Thankful For," on the album *Ideas, Thoughts, and Feelings,* encourages children to think about what they are thankful for and to fill in the pauses in the lyrics. After listening and responding to the song, children can then create a class book or their own individual books.

For a class book, each student should think of one person for whom he or she is thankful. They can each draw a picture and name the person, with the more capable students elaborating about the people chosen. To assemble the book, a pattern can be used, such as:

We have many people to be thankful for.
 Some live near and some live far.
We have many people to be thankful for.
 We will tell you who they are.
(Student's name) is thankful for ————————————.
 (Continue pattern for each student's contribution)
We have many people to be thankful for.
 Some are family and some are friends.
We have many people to be thankful for.
 We love them all and say ''The End.''

Students can also write their own books about the person or persons they appreciate. There are several books that can serve as models for their writing. Kathryn Lasky describes a loved family member in *I Have Four Names for My Grandfather,* which shares a boy's feelings and observations of his grandfather, with black and white photographs by Christopher Knight illustrating the text. *I Love My Baby Sister (Most of the Time)* by Elaine Edelman presents a little girl's description of her new baby sister's good and bad points, with colorful drawings by Wendy Watson. Young writers can personalize the predictable pattern created by Frank Asch in *Just Like Daddy,* in which he tells about a day's activities when a young bear acts ''just like daddy.''

Judy Blume's book *The Pain and The Great One* provides an interesting writing strategy. The book presents two stories, one written by the older sister describing her younger brother, ''The Pain,'' and the other by the brother complaining about his sister, ''The Great One.'' Teachers can share this story with their students and ask the children to pair up. Various combinations of writing roles could be brainstormed in class or predetermined by the teacher for the students. Possible pairs might include:

Brother Bear and Sister Bear describing each other from Stan and Jan Berenstain's series

Ramona and Beezus or Henry and Beezus describing each other from Beverly Cleary's series

Mary and Laura describing each other from Laura Ingalls Wilder's series

Wilbur and Charlotte describing each other based on *Charlotte's Web* by E.B. White

Tom Sawyer and Huckleberry Finn describing each other based on books by Mark Twain

Assigned a character, each student would write about his or her feelings about the other character of the assigned combination. Teachers should urge students to provide informative and positive comments, not just complaints as in the Blume book.

Gift Book

Computer Idea

Teachers and parents can assist children to produce their own stories about someone in their families by using the computer. To set up this bookmaking activity, enter a series of starter sentences similar to the sentences below:

My mom is special because _____.
A favorite time with my mom was when _____.
The silliest thing my mom and I ever did was _____.
My mom's favorite food is _____.
My mom's favorite color is _____.
One thing my mom does better than anyone else is_____.
I love my mom because _____.

You will need to save these beginning lines to disk following the instructions in your word processing manual. After the first child finishes his or her story, you can save the text on file and/or print out the child's work. Then reload the file with the blank starter sentences for the next child. Continue the process for each additional child.

If a child wants to make a book for Grandma, use the "Find and Replace" feature to change each *mom* to *grandma*. Sentences can be added or deleted by each child to personalize the story.

When printing out the children's work, you have two choices. One way would be to print out each child's story on one page, then assemble them all in a class book about their moms or special relatives. The other alternative is to make an individual book for each child by printing out each line of his or her story on separate pages. These pages can then be placed in a blank book or stapled together with a cardboard cover. Let the children illustrate the covers and pages. This idea could be used for creating unique gifts for Mother's or Father's Day, as well as for other holidays.

FRIENDS

Another bookmaking topic that is an important part of your students' lives is friends. Books can be made about friends following many of the strategies mentioned for family books. These books can also be designed as special gifts for family or friends for birthdays or holidays. Children can even make them for classmates in the hospital or moving away.

One writing strategy children can use to make a book about a friend involves pairing words starting with initial letters found in a person's name. For example, a class might want to make a book for their classmate Alexander. They take the letters of the child's name and think of things that could be associated with them by describing the classmate or school. Here is a sample using the acrostic pattern:

A is for *a*ll the fun we have with you at recess.
L is for *l*unch when you share your dessert.
E is for the *e*normous frog you brought for "Show and Tell."
X is for e*x*tra time we got to make this book for you!

Each student could take a letter and draw a picture to be placed on a page of a blank book. Besides using the letters in the student's name, the class might use the letters in the teacher's or the school's name. Favorite jokes or funny anecdotes from the school year can be compiled in similar fashion. This writing strategy using letters and associations can work for a variety of occasions or purposes.

When friends move away, it can be difficult for children to accept. Talking and writing about the experience can help the adjustment. Noah Butler's best friend, Justin, moved away during the summer after first grade, and Katrina Butler wrote down her son's feelings in the song "Justin" (on the album *Abracadabra* by Joe Scruggs). She described the emptiness Noah felt until he realized through a letter from Justin that he was still Justin's best friend, even though they were apart. A similar story is presented in a book by Aliki, *We Are Best Friends*. After listening to the song and reading the story, children can use this pattern to write about their own feelings of loss. They can also include in their book copies of letters they send to and receive from their former classmate, but forever friend.

Books can be written not only about specific people but also about having a family or friends. P.K. Hallinan has published a book, *That's What a Friend Is*, to which children can easily relate because it is written in manuscript printing and includes the author's own drawings. There are several songs about having friends with lyrics that can also inspire writers:

"You Are Special" by Fred Rogers on the album *You Are Special* by Mister Rogers

"I Need You" by Fred Rogers on the album *A Place of Our Own* by Mister Rogers

"A Good Friend" by Rosen, Shontz, and Storey on the album *It's the Truth* by Rosenshontz

"Friendship Song" by Philip Balsam and Dennis Lee on the album *Fraggle Rock* by Henson Associates

"The More We Get Together" Traditional song on the album *Singable Songs for the Very Young* by Raffi

After reading Hallinan's story and listening to the songs, students can think about why friendships are important and generate their own text or lyrics to be written and illustrated in a blank book.

CAREERS

As they consider how important other people are in their lives, we can ask children to describe what they hope to be like as they grow older. They can consider what occupations their parents and other adults have and what they like about those various careers. There are several book styles that can be used to collect children's ideas about future work or roles.

In the book *You Can Be Anything* by Peter Seymour, each page presents a description of a different job that a child might do. To help the children image themselves in the occupations, Carol Wynne designed and illustrated the pages so that one of two cardboard characters, a boy or a girl, can be added to the scene by sliding it into a slot. After reading this book to your class, you can personalize the ideas by encouraging your students to create their own descriptions and drawings of different jobs.

Wynne's book design can be recreated in a blank book by gluing two ribbons inside the book's cover, close to the binding. To the ribbons, attach cardboard figures of a girl and a boy. Add the children's job descriptions and drawings. Then add a strip of paper to each illustration to make a slot in which a figure can fit. Teachers and parents can personalize this bookmaking idea for each child by attaching his or her photograph to the face of the cardboard figure.

The books *If I weren't me...who would I be?* by Pam Adams and *Hey, Look at Me! I Can Be* by Merry Thomasson both use the bookmaking strategy of cutting a hole through each page (see SEPTEMBER — School Routines) and placing a mirror or a child's photograph on the inside of the

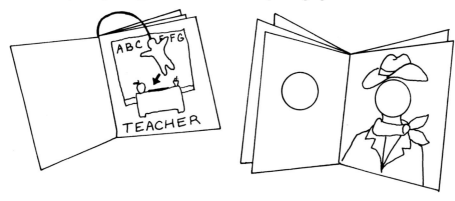

back cover to show through the holes. Then on each page, an illustration is drawn around the hole to include the child's face reflected in the mirror or shown in the photograph. The text describing the job or naming the role is added.

Someday by Charlotte Zolotow offers a predictable pattern that students of all abilities can follow. On each page, the young heroine wishes what someday may happen. Children can also make wishes, such as:

Someday, I'll play baseball for the Chicago Cubs and I will hit a home run
   every game.
Someday, I'm going to fly an airplane and fly around the world.
Someday, I hope to be like my dad with a son like me.

More capable students can elaborate reasons for their wishes. Their dreams can be combined in a book that might even be saved for a future reunion, when the students could see if their early goals were actually achieved.

As mentioned, the books that students produce can also serve as gifts to special friends or relatives. Teachers can use these ideas for creating holiday presents to be given in December. What better way to demonstrate how much they care than to make a book, a gift that can be opened and enjoyed again and again?

December

Gifts, Traditions, and Holidays

During December, gifts are often exchanged among friends and relatives. A handmade book makes an excellent gift because it can be personalized for a loved one. Through its artwork and written text, a book captures the uniqueness of the giver as well as the recipient. Book writing offers the opportunity to record traditions and memories of holidays, such as Christmas, Hanukkah, birthdays, Mother's Day and Father's Day, throughout the year. The following strategies can help bookmakers design special editions which will be cherished in family or school libraries.

GIFTS

At holiday times, home and classroom activities often include making presents to be given. Parents will appreciate the change a handmade book offers from the "juice can" pencil holders and "painted rock" paperweights, while teachers will welcome a child-made book as a gift that doesn't have to be eaten, worn, or put on the wall.

The books students make as gifts may record their own growth or give an account of how the person receiving the gift is special to them. Your students could begin a book about themselves by writing a poem similar to the one designed by Judy Waller, an Indianapolis mother.

> Mama, you're special. I know it's true.
> So I thought I ought to do
> Something special just for you.
> So settle back in a little nook
> And take a look at your own book.

On the inside pages, the students can describe themselves, their feelings, and their favorite things. You may want to provide some of the following ideas as a catalyst:

I am_____inches tall and weigh_____ pounds. I'm the size of a_____.

Here's how far I can stretch my hug. (Tape a piece of yarn the length of the child's arm span to this page in the book.)

This is the shape of my hand. (Draw around hand or make a handprint with tempera paint.)

Here is the way I sign my name. _____

There are lots of things I love.
> My favorite food is_____.
> My favorite color is _____.
> My favorite book is _____

But most of all, I love YOU!

Waller closed her book with the following poem:

> This book was made with love and care
> Because we have so much to share.
> We hope it brought you greatest pleasure
> Because Mamas are our dearest treasure.

Although written when she was helping her children make a book for their grandmother, the same pattern can be adapted to create a book for different relatives on other occasions, such as a birthday, Mother's Day, or Father's Day. Children's original artwork, their own poetry or prose, and their handprints will make this book special to the person receiving it.

For another unique gift book idea, read *A Secret for Grandmother's Birthday* by Franz Brandenberg. In it, two grandchildren reflect on all the different things they love about their grandmother as they prepare for her birthday. The grandson combines all their memories about special times with Grandmother into a poem that becomes his gift. Encourage children to think about a mother, a father, a teacher, or another favorite adult in their lives and to compose a story that tells what makes that person special. Their text could follow a pattern similar to this:

Grandpa, we love your big gold pocket watch.
Grandpa, we love the drives through the country with you.
Grandpa, we love your hugs and kisses.

Cookbook

Computer Idea

To create a cookbook using the computer, a data base program can be helpful in structuring a format for entering favorite recipes. Talk about the concept of "fields" (categories) with your students. Together, create appropriate fields to be used for each recipe. For example,

Type of Food:	Procedure:
Getting Ready:	How It Tastes:
Ingredients:	Contributed by:

Once the fields have been set up using the data base, information for each recipe can be entered and saved. When all the recipes have been entered, they can be sorted into special food categories, such as appetizers, salads, main dishes, and desserts. Recipes can then be printed out in these categories, providing an organizational pattern for the cookbook.

After the recipes have been printed out, they can be mounted in blank books. Original artwork or pictures of different types of food cut from magazines can be used to illustrate. Adhesive tabs could be added, or edges of pages can be cut to create tabs. Half-inch tabs can be created by cutting the book pages along the right-hand side.

A poem can be added as an introduction to the book. Let students create their own, or offer this one for their use:

This book comes to you as a reward
For all the times you've stirred and poured,
mixed and baked, or chopped and stewed
to whip up wonderful food.

New ideas in here are mixed
With favorite dishes that you've fixed.
I think you are a wonderful cook
And hope you enjoy this recipe book.

Ask teachers, administrators, and other school staff to contribute recipes to the class book as well.

Cookbooks make wonderful gifts, too. Students can prepare picture cookbooks for brothers, sisters, or friends that feature one recipe, with each page illustrating one step of the process for preparing that food. The name of the recipe is written on the title page. The first page says, "To make _____, you will need...." Then follows a list of all the ingredients that will be used in the recipe and a picture of each:

two red apples
one stalk of celery
one small box of raisins
two tablespoons of mayonnaise

The rest of the pages give specific directions for each step of the recipe. The last page could show a picture of the prepared food being eaten and have a text that says, "Then eat and enjoy!" For parents, grandparents, or other relatives, children could prepare a book of the class's favorite recipes.

Not only do children enjoy making books as gifts for others, they also like to think, talk, read, and write about gifts they have already gotten or hope to receive. After Christmas, Hanukkah, or a birthday, a child may enjoy putting together a book at home about special gifts received for the occasion and who they were from. Teachers could make a similar book as a gift for a mother-to-be after a baby shower.

Children can create a class book about gifts by first making colorful drawings or cutting out pictures of favorite items from newspaper advertisements or old catalogs. The pictures can then be mounted on index cards or tagboard.

Write the title "WHAT'S INSIDE?" on the first page of a blank book. Then paste envelopes the students have decorated to look like presents or small colored gift bags (the type without a bottom flap) on the front side of each sheet of paper in the book. The cards with pictures of favorite items prepared earlier are tucked into the envelope or bag "packages." Text can be written on pages facing the packages as follows:

TITLE PAGE: WHAT'S INSIDE? by

PAGE ONE: (back of TITLE PAGE)
Here's a shiny package with a ribbon brightly tied.
The tag says it's for *Mary.* Can you guess what's inside?
She wonders if it might be blocks to build a tower tall.
When she opens it, she finds a round and bouncy

PAGE TWO: (decorated envelope with labeled gift tag pasted to page)
Ball (written on back of picture card in envelope)

PAGE THREE: (back of page two)
Here's a red package with a ribbon brightly tied.

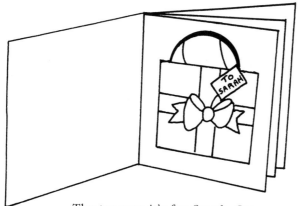

The tag says it's for *Sarah*. Can you guess what's inside?
Maybe it's a sweater or some candy she can eat.
When she opens it, she finds something for her feet.

PAGE FOUR: (decorated envelope with labeled gift tag pasted to page)
Slippers (written on back of picture card in envelope)

CONTINUE by letting children write clues for each gift substituting their own words.

LAST PAGE: (Add a group photo or child's drawing of the class.)
To look inside these packages has been a lot of fun.
But just because they're opened doesn't mean the giving is done.
You may not have much money to buy presents, that is true.
But the very best gift that you can give is really YOU!

TRADITIONS

Gift giving is only one of many traditions practiced at this time of year. Children can make a book to share and record the holiday traditions in their families. Stress that traditions are any practices followed year after year so that children not involved in religious holidays during the month of December will feel comfortable making their contributions to the book.

Before writing, both teachers and students can get a perspective on how holiday traditions have evolved by looking at books about customs, legends, and symbols of holidays around the world. A partial list of good choices includes *Holly, Reindeer, and Colored Lights* by Edna Barth, *The Joys of Christmas* by Kathryn Jackson, and *Light Another Candle: The Story and Meaning of Hanukkah* by Miriam Chaikin.

Help students generate an outline to follow in describing their families' traditions. Here are some questions they might want to consider:

House Decorations - If a Christmas tree is used in your home, how and when is it selected and decorated? How are your tree ornaments, Hanukkah decorations, or other house decorations unique? Where do you hang stockings, lights, or mistletoe? When are decorations put away?

Cards - Does your family send cards? Are they homemade or purchased? When are they sent? How do you enjoy and display cards received?

Gifts - When are gifts purchased or made? How are they wrapped and/or mailed? When are they opened?

Baking - What types of food are made or purchased during this season? When and how does the family participate in making special recipes and meals?

Special Events - Do you attend special programs (i.e., Christmas at the zoo, a madrigal dinner, visits with Santa, musical programs such as *Messiah, Nutcracker,* or school choral recitals)? Save the programs or newspaper advertisements from these events to include in the book.

Religious Observances - Do you attend any special services? Do you light candles on a Hanukkah menorah or Advent wreath? Are there certain prayers said this time of year?

Music - What special songs are used during this season? What are your favorites? Include some of the lyrics in your book.

Children's artwork can illustrate the book. They may also wish to include pictures from greeting cards, magazines, or wrapping paper, and photographs. If you don't have time to use this bookmaking idea in your classroom, suggest that families do it together during holiday break. They can prepare extra editions of their book for other relatives. To accompany the book, they can record family voices reading the text with holiday music playing in the background.

HOLIDAYS

Holiday activities are special not just in December, but throughout the year. Encourage children to create a book that captures a variety of holiday memories. Here is a suggested pattern:

TITLE PAGE: HOLIDAY MEMORIES

PAGE TWO: NEW YEAR'S DAY (Include large picture drawn by child of confetti, horns, streamers, etc.)

PAGE THREE: (Child's name) celebrates New Year's Day by _____.

PAGE FOUR: VALENTINE'S DAY (Include large heart picture drawn by child.)

PAGE FIVE: (Child's name) celebrates Valentine's Day by _____.

Continue this pattern with holidays celebrated each month.

LAST PAGE: (Child's name) celebrates each holiday in a special way.

Take a humorous approach to holidays by reading *Silly Goose and the Holidays* by Bill Martin, Jr. In this book, Silly Goose mixes up his holiday wishes at each celebration. Use a similar predictable pattern to create a book with greeting cards made or collected by students. A glue stick or rubber cement can be used to mount cards on the pages in a blank book in the positions indicated below. For an alternate bookmaking style, try the envelope book described in the Valentine's Day section of the month of FEBRUARY. Invent a text appropriate for the cards chosen. For example,

TITLE PAGE: HOLIDAY MIX-UP

PAGE TWO: (Leave back of title page blank.)

PAGE THREE: On Thanksgiving, I got a very scary card with ghosts and witches on it from my cousin.

PAGE FOUR: Oh, excuse me, that was for Halloween!
(Include Halloween card.)

PAGE FIVE: For Christmas, I got a cute card with a picture of a turkey from Grandma and Grandpa.

PAGE SIX: Oh, excuse me, that was for Thanksgiving! (Include Thanksgiving card.)

Continue this pattern for each holiday.

December allows young authors to create gifts, record memories, and learn about holidays through bookmaking. By reading and making books about gifts, traditions, and holidays, students can gain a greater understanding of what each special celebration means to them.

Note: Teachers can ask parents to save the past year's calendars so children can use pictures from them when writing about their personal histories in May.

January

Animals, Habitats, and Winter

The month of January can be bleak and dreary for children stuck inside all day. Through writing, students can create sunny days and exciting adventures that can help them escape the cold weather. Writing allows a person to be anyone, live anywhere, and do anything. To help children "bear" January's weather, how about encouraging them to make books about animals, habitats, and winter?

ANIMALS

Animals are a favorite topic for authors and artists. Whether the animals are in the home, on the farm, or in the zoo, children are naturally curious to learn about them: what they eat, what they do, and how they grow. Children also enjoy imagining that the animals talk and play just like they do. To assist students in designing their own stories, teachers and parents can read aloud books about animals that can be a springboard for children's imagination or a source of background information.

Dear Zoo, by Rod Campbell, presents a story about a child who writes the zoo to get a pet. No pet delivered is right, though, until finally the child receives a dog. On each page, the reader must lift up a flap representing the mailing container to see what animal is sent. This pattern can be replicated using other animals, another source for the animals, or different descriptions of each animal. One example for a new text might be:

> I asked my mom and dad for a pet.
> They said they'd get me a goldfish.
> "I can't hold it," I said, and I asked them again.
> They said they'd get me a turtle.
> "I can't take it for a walk," I said, and I asked them again.
> (Continue the pattern until the right pet is suggested and
>   conclude the story.)
> "I love it for a pet!" I said, and they gave it to me.

Flaps covering the animal pictures can be added to the pages to encourage the children to predict what is underneath the flap as they read.

Children can also use flaps to make a riddle book about their pets. Each child could describe his or her pet on a flap covering the picture and name of the pet on the page. An individual book can be written about each child's pet including specific details: the animal's name, size, appearance, age, diet, schedule, and needs, and funny incidents involving it. Children can illustrate their books with drawings or photographs.

Joke books about animals can be written by children after they have heard jokes from Bennett Cerf's *Book of Animal Riddles* or one of the "Make Me Laugh" series:

Dumb Clucks! by Rick and Ann Walton, contains jokes about chickens
Elephants Never Forget! by Diane L. Burns contains jokes about elephants
Going Buggy! by Peter and Connie Roop contains jokes about insects
Something's Fishy! by Rick and Ann Walton contains jokes about sea
    creatures

The students can compile their favorite jokes or write their own animal jokes to place in a blank book. Flaps can be employed to cover the answers to the riddles.

There are other books that encourage children to imagine new ideas about animals. Author Judi Barrett and illustrator Ron Barrett create humor in their book *Animals should definitely not wear clothing,* which shows how difficult it would be for a porcupine to wear a dress or an egg-laying hen to wear pants. Children could come up with other animals in ridiculous clothing. Barretts' second book, *Animals should definitely not act like people,* also offers a start for further writing.

Kees Moerbeek's book *Have You Seen a POG?* creates a challenging pop-up book design for bookmakers to try. On each double-page spread is a pop-up face of a different animal, with a description of what the animal says along the top of the spread and what the animal does on the bottom. The center of the page is cut horizontally so the reader can mix and match the descriptions and faces of the animals on the top and bottom half pages to create new combinations, such as a "POG," which is the cross between a pig and a dog. For added help creating the pop-up faces, consult chapter 2 of Joan Irvine's book, *How to Make Pop-Ups*.

Whether in a story or a song, a rhythmic text can offer writers a pattern for adaptation. For example, Bill Martin's story *Brown Bear, Brown Bear, What Do You See?* provides a predictable pattern that can be modified for a variety of uses. The repetitional text pairs questions and answers about different animals. At the end of the book, the reader names all animals seen.

Animal Book

Computer Idea

The computer can help produce a new version of the *Brown Bear, Brown Bear* pattern entitled *Who Do You See?* Using paper or a word processing program, children can create a repetitive text. They can then illustrate their stories using a graphics program.

To start, encourage students to experiment with the text to create their own versions on the *Brown Bear* pattern. Here is one possibility:

Black ant, black ant, who do you see?
I see a yellow chick following me.
Yellow chick, yellow chick, who do you see?
I see a red hen following me.

Continue this pattern and then end the story with:

Animals, animals, who do you see?
I see_____'s class following me.
That's who I see.

To illustrate the *Who Do You See?* book with the computer, children can select a graphics program and an input device, such as the keyboard, a graphics tablet, a mouse, or a joystick, to draw animals for their stories. The choice will depend on hardware, software, and the amount of time available, as well as how much computer experience they have had.

The young illustrator may want to choose one of the drawing programs, *Koala Painter*^{TM} or *Dazzle Draw*^{TM}. Both programs offer children the use of built-in (or pre-made) shapes like circles and rectangles. *Koala Painter* requires the use of the Koala Pad^{TM} as an input device for graphics and has an accompanying disc, *Graphics Exhibitor*^{TM}, to enable the artist to add text to the pictures. *Dazzle Draw* can receive input from a joystick, a mouse, or the Koala Pad and place the text on graphics as part of its program.

For students with previous computer experience, a program like *Logo Writer*^{TM} or *Delta Draw*^{TM} could be used. In these programs that use the keyboard for input, basic shapes must be drawn once by the student, but can be saved to be used repeatedly in a variety of pictures.

A helpful hint when time is limited on the computer is to ask the children to first draw their animals on paper. The sketches can then be used as models for their computer drawings. Young illustrators can consult Ed Emberley's *Drawing Book of Animals,* which demonstrates how to create animals from basic shapes. Printing programs, such as *SuperPrint!*^{TM}, *Print Shop*^{TM}, and *Printmaster Plus*^{TM}, offer the use of ready-made animal art and only require a keyboard for input.

Using storybook characters, another adaptation similar to the sample computer story, *Who Do I See?,* could be designed, for example, Curious George, Curious George, who do you see? (*Curious George,* by H.A. Rey). Teachers or students can add illustrations of the characters they select to create an easy-to-read book. This book pattern also helps children review stories and characters.

A book about friends and relatives could be made by families using names of people instead of animals or characters:

Mary, Mary, who do you see?
I see Grandmother looking at me.

Continue through other people and end with:

I see Mary looking at me.
Mary, Mary, who do you see?
I see Grandmother, Uncle...(list all names) at Christmas.
That's who I see.

If it includes a photograph and a brief description about each person, this book can help children remember family members or friends who visit once a year. A personalized version can create a special holiday or birthday gift for a child by starting the book with his or her name.

With this text pattern, children can write a book using specific vocabulary associated with that time of year. For instance, at Halloween, start with the following text:

> Black cat, black cat, what do you spy?
> I spy an evil bat that's ready to fly.
> Evil bat, evil bat, why do you fly?

Continue rhyming pattern.

Children enjoy matching adjectives to describe the nouns or finding an appropriate verb to keep the rhythm and the rhyme. Foreign language teachers can use this bookmaking pattern to assist their students to learn a new language.

Songs can also provide a catalyst for more writing. After listening to the traditional song "Baa, Baa, Black Sheep," Raffi, on his album, *The Corner Grocery Store,* recorded his new song, "Cluck, Cluck Red Hen." He wrote new lyrics to the "Black Sheep" song using different animals, such as a hen, a cow, and a bee. Children can add more verses using other animals and the predictable question-answer pattern:

> Neigh, neigh, brown horse,
> have you a ride for me?
> Yes sir, yes sir, anytime you please.
> One in the morning, another at noon,
> One in the evening underneath the moon...

Illustrations and the music can accompany the text to make a songbook.

Rosenshontz offers another song for which children love to create more verses — "I wish I Was" on their *Tickles You!* album. They think of different animals they would like to be. Students can prepare other rhyming wishes, for instance,

> I'd like to be a mouse.
> I'd run around the house.
> I'd like to be, I'd like to be,
> I'd like to be a mouse.

To illustrate each verse chosen, a child can look for a specific animal picture in magazines and add a photograph of himself or herself to cover the animal's face so that the wish comes true.

Factual stories can be written after reading books on a particular subject. For instance, children can write books about spiders after listening to stories such as *Charlotte's Web* by E.B. White, *The Lady and the Spider* by Faith McNulty, or *The Very Busy Spider* by Eric Carle. Students can learn a variety of information about spiders from these stories. They can then substantiate the facts gleaned from their reading in an encyclopedia or another reference book, such as *Spider's Web* by Christine Back and Barrie Watts. Teachers can reverse this reading-writing strategy by asking the children to research about another animal and then to write a fictitious story using the information collected.

Children are naturally curious about animals, and that curiosity can be channeled into writing factual books or fictional stories about animals as personal pets, in playful puns, or in patterned texts. Flaps, pop-up pages, rhymes, and music can all assist the writer to compose a fun and exciting book. A classroom nature library can be written with each child preparing a book on a different animal. There are endless possibilities for creating animal books, and January is a long month with lots of time for such creativity.

HABITATS

Where animals and people call home is another topic for bookmaking. Do they live in a nest or a cave, in a tent or an apartment, by water or a mountain? With whom do they live? What's their neighborhood like? Have they lived anywhere else?

To help your students start writing, share the book *A House Is a House for Me* by Mary Ann Hoberman, and begin a discussion about the various homes for animals, people, and even objects. Children can brainstorm the different homes possible, and each may select one to describe and illustrate for a factual book. One book could be about nests and the different animals who make their homes in them, or one could be about houses and the different ways people build them in the students' own city, throughout the country, or even around the world. Peter Spier's book *People* may help writers consider how and where people live.

Children can easily describe their own homes and neighborhoods. In a small blank book turned horizontally, with the binding on the top, a student can decorate the cover to look like the front of his or her home, then on the inside pages, describe the different rooms, including any area that is just his

or her own. In a large blank book, students can describe their school neighborhood, complete with a map drawn of the area. They could include the history of the neighborhood and how it has changed. Information can be gathered from older residents or the city records. Descriptions of parts of the neighborhood, such as nearby stores, the school, a fire station, or parks, could be added.

If they have ever moved, students can describe their former homes. What were they like — any similarities or differences? Children might imagine where they would move if they had a choice. Teachers can assist by adapting the pattern John Burningham uses in his book *Would You Rather....* to develop prompting questions. For example, children might be asked whether they would like to live in a warm, moderate, or cold climate; by an ocean, a lake, or a river; or in a city, a town, or the country. Each set of options could be placed on a double-page spread in a large blank book to serve as the prewriting experience.

Although children can dream about living someplace else, they often have to move where they do not wish. Marjorie Weinman Sharmat presents this issue in her book *Gila monsters meet you at the airport*. In it, a boy describes why he doesn't want to move to Arizona, based on his misconceptions about that area of the country. This book can provide a model for creating books about other places. For instance, a child might write

> I don't want to move to California because there everyone
> - has a deep tan (I don't tan. I just freckle and burn.)
> - goes surfing in the ocean waves (I can't even swim well.)
> - has straight blond hair (Mine's red and naturally curly.)

Then after students write what they think about other places, they could research by reading geography books, writing to Chamber of Commerces, and picking up travel brochures. Possibly pen pals could be arranged so students could compare their ideas about another place with what the area is actually like.

Homes for animals and people can be the subject for a variety of books. These book can help students learn about each other, as well as about animals.

WINTER

Winter's cold creates time for making books because it forces students to spend more time indoors. Children can have fun designing various types of books using winter as the theme.

One winter activity is to make and look at tracks in the snow. To help children learn to discriminate between different animal tracks, teachers might like to share *How to Be an Animal Detective,* story by Millicent

Selsam and pictures by Ezra Jack Keats. After looking at the book, students can make their own guidebook using ink pads and fingerprints to illustrate the tracks.

Telling stories by the fire is another winter experience that can help to create books. In *The Mitten,* Alvin Tresselt retells an old Ukrainian folktale about different animals seeking shelter from the cold. Each animal squeezes into a boy's lost mitten laying in the forest, until the mitten bursts. Children can rewrite this tale in more contemporary style in a blank book. They can cut out forms of a mitten from construction paper and mount one on each page. Different animals who try to get inside the mittens for comfort can be illustrated and stuffed into the mitten openings with the last picture showing the mitten in pieces and the animals running away.

Indoor games can be played with family or friends to help the winter pass. One game can be adapted from the book *Puniddles* by Bruce and Brett McMillan, in which students must deduce from two pictures the "punny" compound word. For example, pages might include pictures of the following pairs with the resulting word(s) on the backs of the pages.
Possible winter combinations:

Ice	Cream	Ice cream
Snow	Man	Snowman
Foot	Prints	Footprints

Possible animal combinations:

Bear	Feet	Bare feet
Cow	Boy	Cowboy
Horse	Shoe	Horseshoe

Each child can contribute a set of words and pictures to create a book full of language play.

Other winter indoor activities can also be the focus of a book. Just as the television episode about "Tight Times and Free Things to Do," from the series "Reading Rainbow," shared free or inexpensive ideas for summer fun, students can also dream up ways to have fun indoors when the weather outside is inclement. Assemble their ideas into a handbook of things to do when the class can't go outside for recess and when students have to say indoors after lunch.

Whether students are writing about animals, habitats, or winter, challenge them to create books that will be useful or fun — or both!

February

Valentine's Day, Presidents' Day, and Dental Health Month

February adds life to winter with special events like Valentine's Day, Presidents' Day, and Dental Health Month. Valentine's Day gives a chance to expand card exchanges and letter writing into a bookmaking experience. Presidents' Day activities can interest students in researching and writing about famous people. In addition, this month is a good time to make books that reinforce health concepts, such as taking good care of teeth. The following bookmaking ideas will help you celebrate the special days of February.

VALENTINE'S DAY

This month, students look forward to sending, as well as receiving, valentines. Students often have leftover valentines from boxes purchased for classroom exchanges. Teachers can encourage students to use those extra cards or valentines they have received in some of the following bookmaking projects.

A valentine riddle book can be made using the cards. For instance, for a valentine showing a picture of Alice in Wonderland, the riddle might read,

"Who followed a white rabbit down a hole?" In a blank book, a student can write a riddle on the front side of a page and put the card with the answer on the back side of the page.

The computer can be used to print the text of a personalized rhyming book illustrated with child-made or purchased valentines. Students in intermediate classrooms might enjoy making the books to share with younger children in primary grades.

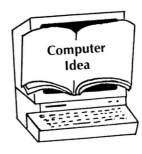

Ten Little Valentines

Computer Idea

To create a valentine counting book for each child in the classroom, first use a word processor to enter the following valentine poem, or your class's own variation, into the computer, substituting the name of one child in your class for each *Laura*. Fill in the other blanks by writing names of that child's friends, relatives, or teacher.

Ten Little Valentines

Ten little valentines that *Laura* nearly signed,
    she sent one to _____,
    and now there are nine.

Nine little valentines, none of them are late,
    Laura sent one to _____,
    and now there are eight.

Eight little valentines waiting to be given,
    Laura sent one to _____,
    and now there are seven.

Seven little valentines that *Laura* worked to fix,
    she sent one to _____,
    and now there are six.

Six little valentines anxious to arrive,
    Laura sent one to _____,
    and now there are five.

Five little valentines waiting by the door,
    Laura sent one to _____,
    and now there are four.

Four little valentines as you can plainly see,
   Laura sent one to _____,
   and now there are three.

Three little valentines all bright and new,
   Laura sent one to_____,
   and now there are two.

Two little valentines having lots of fun,
   Laura sent one to _____,
   and now there is just one.

One little valentine, staying here to say:
   HAVE A HAPPY VALENTINE'S DAY!
   Save or print out the first child's personalized version of the poem. Then use "find and replace" (check your word processing manual if you're not sure how to do this) to change that child's name to the name of another student in the classroom. Save or print out that child's poem, and repeat for each child in the class. Text can be printed out on wide self-adhesive labels and stuck into blank books, or printed on regular paper, cut apart, and then pasted into the book.

   Pages can be illustrated with students' drawings, computer graphics, child-made or purchased valentines, heart potato stamps, or actual photos of people receiving the valentines.

Children become more aware of the value of exchanging correspondence as Valentine's Day approaches. Janet and Allan Ahlberg's book *The Jolly Postman or Other People's Letters* highlights various functions of letter writing. In this story, a postman delivers an assortment of mail to favorite fairy tale characters, including an apology letter from Goldilocks to Baby Bear, a catalog from a supply house to the Wicked Witch, a vacation postcard from Jack to the Giant, and a preview copy of a picture book from a publisher to Cinderella. At each house, the postman drinks a cup of tea before going on.

Bound between the pages of the book are envelopes that hold the various pieces of mail. After reading the story, students enjoy imagining and writing about other characters who might receive mail and the types of messages they might get. In one student's version, a mailman eats a cookie at each stop, and gets rounder and rounder as he continues his deliveries.

To assemble a book of this style, envelopes can be attached to the pages of a blank book with rubber cement or a glue stick. Cards, letters, or pictures related to the story are then tucked inside the envelopes.

For a bookmaking challenge, make the pages of a blank book into envelopes. To create a small blank book of six envelopes, follow these directions:

1. Number the sheets from one to fourteen lightly in pencil (to be erased later).

2. Measure a horizontal line 3 inches from the top of sheet #3, and cut on the line all the way across, removing the top 3 inches from the sheet.

3. On sheet #2, cut down 3 inches from the top of the page along the bound edge. Now fold this sheet over sheet #3, thus creating a flap.

4. To create a triangle-shaped flap similar to one on a normal envelope flap, measure 2¾ inches in from the edge of the book along the bottom of the flap and mark a point. With a straight edge, make lines from the point to the upper corners of the flap. Cut along the lines.

5. On sheet #3, lightly trace around the flap created with sheet #2. Cut a triangle from sheet #3 slightly smaller than the one traced. With rubber cement, glue together just the side and bottom edges of sheets #2 and #3.

6. Repeat process to create six envelopes, leaving sheets #1 and #14 as whole sheets.

1.
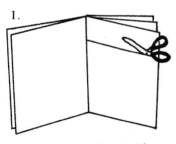
Number sheets from 1-14 in pencil. Cut three inches off top of sheet three.

2.
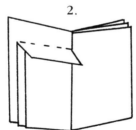
Cut along bound edge of sheet two. Fold top down over sheet three.

3.
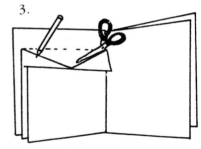
Draw and cut triangle-shaped flap on sheet two.

4.
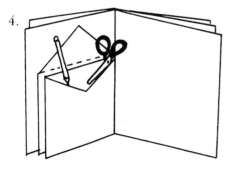
Draw and cut a smaller triangle-shaped flap on sheet three.

5.
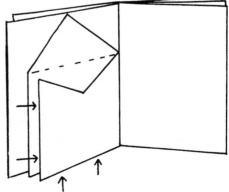
Glue edges of sheets two and three along bottom and outside edge to complete the envelope.

For a large blank book with six envelopes, follow the directions above with these two exceptions: In step #4, cut just the corners off the flap to simulate a large mailing envelope. In step #5, it is not necessary to trace and cut out a triangle slightly smaller than the flap.

Using this envelope style and a blank book with the "Busy Bears" or "Animal Parade" cover, children could address envelopes and write messages to bears in stories they have read. Here are some sample ideas:

To Paddington (*A Bear Called Paddington* by Michael Bond):
A postcard from his aunt in darkest Peru

To Corduroy (*Corduroy* by Don Freeman):
A namecard for his new pocket from Lisa

To Little Bear (*Little Bear* by Else Minarik):
A recipe for Birthday soup from Mother Bear

To Brother Bear (*Bike Lesson* by Stan and Jan Berenstain):
A manual of rules to remember from Papa Bear

To Winnie-the-Pooh (*The House at Pooh Corners* by A.A. Milne):
A shopping list with the reminder - "Don't forget the honey!"

To a favorite teddy bear:
A letter from your students

On the last page, position the following text so that it shows above each envelope:

And then the letter carrier reached into the mailbag
and found a letter for:

Next glue a small envelope on the last page, which will be hidden by the other envelopes in the book. Written on the outside of the envelope is the word YOU! Inside is a card that reads "The End."

For another variation using the envelope-style book, brainstorm for ideas of valentines that one famous character might send to another, such as:

A funny note from Curious George to the man with the
yellow hat (*Curious George* by H.A. Rey).
A romantic love letter from Prince Charming to Cinderella
A cute valentine from Christopher Robin to Winnie-the-Pooh
An affectionate message from George Washington to Martha

An alternate way to customize this blank book is to cut the inside pages to form half of a heart shape so that when the book is open, each double-page spread forms a heart. Paste red construction paper to the end covers with rubber cement or a glue stick so the white heart will stand out.

PRESIDENTS' DAY

Close to Presidents' Day, discuss with children what makes someone famous, and people they can think of who are famous. Have children draw or cut out faces of famous people, including George Washington and Abraham Lincoln. *Draw 50 Famous Faces* by Lee Ames may help students get started with their illustrations. While children's own drawings will be the most powerful, you may wish to have some clip art available for them to use to supplement their own pictures. Students draw or mount one famous personality on each page of a blank book with the text:

This famous face belongs to _____.

On the last page (inside back cover), use epoxy to mount a small unbreakable mirror so that the reader will see his or her own reflection with the text.

This face belongs to me! It isn't famous — YET!

This book is an adaptation of one that teacher Jackie McVey designed to use with children in her kindergarten class.

To challenge more advanced students with a Presidents' Day activity, let each child research a different president. Make resources such as encyclopedias and biographies available. Visit the school or public library for additional information if desired. Generate a list of questions to be answered about each president. This will be most effective if done as a class project. Questions students come up with may include:

When was this president born?
When did this president die?
What did this president look like?
When was the term of office?
What hobbies did this president have?
What important things happened during this presidency?
Was this person a good president? Why or why not?

Have students write their questions on index cards (one question per card) and then answer each question in a complete sentence. Each student can arrange his or her cards in the sequence that would make the best story. Students could also write the names of the answer sources on the cards, to be transferred later to bibliography pages in their books.

A student forms a biographical sketch of the president she or he researched by copying the statements used to answer the questions onto another piece of paper and adding appropriate transitional sentences. After several editing sessions, students can make final copies of their presidential biographies and illustrate them in blank books. A class book could also be made, with one or two pages devoted to each president researched.

The same organizational structure used to write reports on presidents can be used in writing other biographies. Authors, sports heroes, television celebrities, and movie stars all make interesting people for your students' biographical books. The list of questions should be customized to fit the subject. Authors' circles could be formed, with students grouped together according to the occupations of the famous people they chose. Students can then share their lists of questions with each other and get more ideas from their classmates. If students choose living persons for their biographies, they can write letters to those celebrities to ask questions that books or periodicals don't answer.

DENTAL HEALTH MONTH

February is Dental Health Month. After listening to Raffi's adaptation of the song "Brush Your Teeth" on the album *Singable Songs for the Very Young,* use the traditional lyrics as the text for a book:

When you wake up in the morning, and it's quarter to one,
And you want to have a little fun,
REFRAIN:
You brush your teeth — Ch, ch, ch, ch, ch, ch, ch, ch, ch.
You brush your teeth — Ch, ch, ch, ch, ch, ch, ch, ch, ch.

When you wake up in the morning, and it's quarter to two,
And you just don't know what to do,
REFRAIN

When you wake up in the morning, and it's quarter to three,
You want the biggest smile for me,
REFRAIN

When you wake up in the morning, it's quarter to four,
You hear a great big knock on your door,
REFRAIN

When you wake up in the morning, it's quarter to five,
You're so happy to be alive,
REFRAIN

Add a verse of your own, such as

When you wake up in the morning, it's quarter to six,
And you see your dog doing some tricks,
REFRAIN

Use the first page of a blank book as a title page. Cut a three-inch strip off the bottom of each of the other pages. On the bottom three inches of the inside back cover, put a smiling mouth with teeth showing and the words to

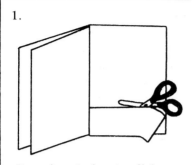

1. Cut a three-inch strip off the bottom of all pages except first page (use as a title page).

2. On the inside back cover, draw a smiling mouth with the teeth showing.

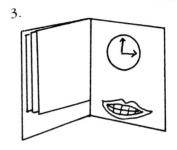

3. Glue small cardboard clock on inside of back cover.

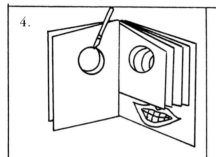

4. Cut a hole through the front cover and all inside pages so the clock face shows.

5. On each front page, write in verses. Write refrain near mouth.

6. Optional: Attach a toothbrush to the book with string or dental floss.

the refrain. Mount a small cardboard clock (available at teacher supply stores) on the inside back cover. Using a good-quality matte knife, cut a hole through the inside pages and the front cover so the clock shows through. Write one verse on the front side of each of the remaining pages. Poke a hole through the cover, close to the binding. Thread a piece of string or dental floss through the hole in the book, then tie to the hole in the handle of a toothbrush.

Brochures produced by your state dental association provide material that can be cut apart to create informative books on dental health. Often the brochures may have a reading level too difficult for some students, but the teacher and class can use the information and pictures to help them write and illustrate an easier book on the same subject. Following this strategy, pamphlets from the Red Cross, the American Medical Association, the Dairy Council, the Board of Health, and other organizations can be used to make books on other topics, such as nutrition, pollution, and poison.

To create a poison awareness book, first check with poison control centers or local drugstores to see if there is a special poison symbol in your state. If so, you may want to incorporate it when making your book. In Indiana, Hooks Drug Stores give free stickers of ''Mr Yuk''™, a character young children learn quickly to recognize as marking poison substances. Personalize the story text by filling in the blanks with the names of your children or the names of students in your class:

TITLE PAGE: (Teacher's name) says NO! A Story about Safety

PAGE TWO: _____is thirsty, and sees something that is his favorite color. Can he drink it?

PAGE THREE: (Teacher's name) says NO!
         It's (custodian)'s window cleaner.

PAGE FOUR: _____sees something white on a little brush. Can she use it to brush her teeth?

PAGE FIVE: (Teacher's name) says NO!
         It's correction fluid we use to white out mistakes.

Continue the pattern using other poison items. Then end with:

   The students see hot dogs, fruit, and green beans.
   Can they eat them?

   (Teacher's name) says YES!
   ''It's time for lunch!''

Stickers or drawings of a familiar poison symbol and children's artwork or pictures cut from pamphlets or magazines can be used for illustrations.

   Now students have taken a look at the past by writing presidential biographies, at the present by exploring correspondence, and at their own futures by becoming more aware of the importance of maintaining good health.

March

Past, Present, and Future

In March, allow your children to daydream about the past, the present, and the future by creating stories for books. To accomplish this time travel, students can think about prehistoric dinosaurs, everyday experiences, and space adventures.

PAST

March into spring with dinosaurs! Kids enjoy learning about the large, funny-shaped animals who once roamed their neighborhoods. They like to imagine what it would be like to be a dinosaur or to have one as a pet. Use this as a ''spring'' board for bookmaking this month.

To assist students, teachers will find it helpful to read some books about the different kinds of dinosaurs that lived during prehistoric time. Check the library for books or purchase paperbacks to add to your home or classroom library, such as:

Dinosaur Time by Peggy Parish
Dinosaurs by Peter Zallinger
Digging Up Dinosaurs by Aliki
Dinosaurs and More Dinosaurs by M. Jean Craig

Based on the information learned about dinosaurs, children may want to make a dictionary of dinosaur words explaining the Greek language roots (i.e., *deinos* means terrible and *sauros* means lizard). They can also make a book on the different kinds of dinosaurs. Teachers may ask the students to select a dinosaur and describe it. To illustrate their work, children can consult Michael Emberley's book *Dinosaurs!* or trace Trend Enterprises' "Dinosaur Stencils." Their papers can be combined into a reference book for the class. The large blank book with the dinosaur on the cover can be used for bookmaking.

Songs can be written that describe dinosaurs, such as the songs on the two albums *Our Dinosaur Friends* (Early Years or Intermediate Years) by Art Barduhn and Pam Johnson. Other body motions and music to accompany the lyrics can also be created.

Children can design imaginative songs and books about dinosaurs. For example, after listening to the song "If I Brought a Dinosaur Home," from the album *Reading Rainbow Songs,* with music by Steve Horelick and lyrics by Dennis Kleinman and Janet Weir, the students can consider what would happen if they brought a dinosaur or another strange animal home. The book *If the dinosaurs came back* by Bernard Most offers a predictable pattern for classroom reading and writing by asking the children to imagine dinosaurs living in the twentieth century.

Your students will enjoy learning "punny" dinosaur riddles from the book *Tyrannosaurus Wrecks* by Noelle Sterne, and they can create new jokes for their own version. They can have fun thinking of different verses for the humorous song "Please Don't Bring Your Tyrannosaurus to Show and Tell," from the album *Late Last Night* by Joe Scruggs.

Teachers can offer their students a writing game by using the "chain story" idea from the book *The Tyrannosaurus Game* by Steven Kroll. At the classroom writing center, ask your students to take turns telling a dinosaur story. A timer can be used to help pace the children. Children could either dictate their stories or take turns writing. Here's how it might work. The first student would start the story and write for five minutes. The next student would be allowed time to read the first student's writing (or the first student would read his or her work to the second). Then the second student would write for five minutes, continuing the story where the first student left off. This process would continue until the last student ends the story. The chain story, or round-robin writing strategy, works well for other topics and for computer usage.

Dinosaur Book

Dinosaur Days^{TM} allows students to design a computer picture from the days of the dinosaur by choosing backgrounds, heads, necks, bodies, legs, tails, and miscellaneous props. Backgrounds and body parts range from the whimsical to the realistic. Graphics from other software packages in the Pelican® Software's *Creative Writing Series* can be used with *Dinosaur Days* as well. Creations can be printed out in the designer's choice of five different sizes. The program will print color on an Imagewriter II.®

Once the picture is drawn, it may be printed or saved before going on to write a story. The "Dinosaur Diary" portion of the program lets students write a few sentences or a full screen story to describe their picture. Features of the "Diary" allow insertion and deletion of text, but do not include more sophisticated word processing features, such as moving or replacing text.

One way to use the program would be for each student in the class to design a dinosaur and then write a story about it. Printouts could be pasted into a large blank book with the "Dinosaur" cover. If pictures are printed in the small size, dinosaur stories can be written and illustrated in comic book style. A dinosaur could be printed in all the five sizes available to create a book about a dinosaur who changes size.

If computer access is limited, print out and make copies of a variety of dinosaur parts on blank backgrounds. Let students cut them apart and arrange them to make their own dinosaur pictures. They can create stories to accompany their illustrations.

Dinosaur Days also includes a picture data base with lots of information about dinosaurs that children could use to write their own dinosaur encyclopedia. Pictures and text from the data base can be printed out so students can take information back to their desks for reference.

PRESENT

The books students make should include selections that portray their everyday lives. In years to come, they will enjoy reading about their childhood days. Young authors can also have fun imagining adventures to create unusual days.

Good days are wonderful and should be cherished. For instance, a child can make a book that includes all the details of his or her team winning the basketball tournament, the swim meet, or a gymnastic competition. A small blank book with the "Sports" cover, can be filled with descriptions of the games played, the team members, the coach, and final events. Photographs, programs, and newspaper clippings can be used to illustrate the book.

In cloudy March, days may also be shadowed with disappointments. Reading books about other children's bad days may help your students to see humor in these situations and become inspired to write about their own horrible days. Two books that describe less-than-perfect days are Judith Viorst's *Alexander and the Terrible, Horrible, No Good, Very Bad Day* and Patricia Giff's *Today Was a Terrible Day*. After sharing these books, ask your students to list everything that went wrong for them on bad days and to write their own stories describing these different mishaps. Have the students add humor by exaggerating their woes.

Children can combine their good-day/bad-day ideas and create another book. Remy Charlip uses this contrasting pattern in the book *Fortunately*. Students can follow this organization by first writing something that went right, such as

Fortunately, it was windy enough outside to fly kites.

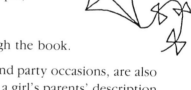

Then they can add what went wrong, for example,

Unfortunately, my kite had a hole in it.

This repetitive pattern can be continued through the book.

Memories of special days, such as birthdays and party occasions, are also worth saving in books. Cynthia Rylant presents a girl's parents' description of her first six birthdays in her book *Birthday Presents*. Encourage your students to reflect on their past birthdays to remember how the days were celebrated to create their own books.

Another special activity for children is to sleep over at a friend's house. Can they recall the first time they stayed overnight away from home? Share Bernard Waber's book *Ira Sleeps Over* to help children think about how they could describe their experiences.

Ordinary, everyday experiences also make interesting subjects for bookmaking. Children can cut up advertisements and product labels to create a book about environmental print. Emerging readers and writers will delight in recognizing the print they are familiar with in their lives, and more capable learners can analyze the presentation and selection of the printed labels to create their own new labels.

Several books about children's daily life can offer a springboard for young writers to design sequels. For example, students can write another adventure for Beverly Cleary's Ramona Quimby or Robert McCloskey's Homer Price. They may also enjoy designing a new mystery for Donald Sobol's Encyclopedia Brown to solve.

Books that cause children to laugh at ordinary activities include the "Amelia Bedelia" series by Peggy Parish. In each story, Amelia is given directions that she misunderstands because she takes an expression literally or confuses exact word meanings. For instance, if she is asked to dust the furniture, she throws dirt around the room because they did not ask her to "un-dust" the furniture. Children can make up their own books about Amelia Bedelia and include confusing directions.

Unusual days can challenge students' imaginations. What if they woke up with antlers, as in *Imogene's Antlers* by David Small, started to shrink, as in *Shrinking Treehorn* by Forence Heide, or were flattened by a bulletin board, as in *Flat Stanley* by Jeff Brown? Children can imagine what they would do in similar situations and create new adventures.

In *The Snail's Spell,* Joanne Ryder asks readers to wonder what they would experience if they became as small as a snail crawling in a garden. Other animals and situations can be substituted to design new tales. *Once, Said Darlene* by William Sleator presents a girl who repeatedly tells outlandish tales that her friends disbelieve, except for one boy. His belief in her stories helps to break an evil spell and allows the girl to return to the make-believe world she described. Children can create new similar stories about spells and imagination.

FUTURE

Science fiction and space adventures offer bookmakers an infinite number of writing possibilities. Whether describing travel throughout the galaxy or a creature from another planet, stories can be created that allow students to expand their imaginations.

Space stories can be written as sequels to published books. For instance, young children delight in the crazy experiences of Alistair in *Alistair in Outer Space* and *Alistair's Time Machine* by Marilyn Sadler. Older students will enjoy reading about Eddie and his space friend, Marty, in Louis Slobodkin's "The Amazing Space Ship Adventures" series. Young writers can use either the same characters or the same plot lines to create new adventures. The "Creatures" small blank book provides a decorative cover for bookmakers' use.

The reader-response bookmaking strategy is perfect for designing a space story, such as *Choose Your Own Adventure: Space and Beyond* by R.A. Montgomery. First, the writer describes the setting for the book and two options from which the reader must choose to continue the story:

You are walking to school one morning when suddenly a spaceship lands in front of you and the door opens —

If you decide to run for safety, turn to page two.
If you decide to investigate the spaceship, turn to page four.

Then the writer describes the situation and proposes two more choices. More and more situations and options are created as the story continues, until various endings are supplied.

To keep track of the different choices available in the adventure book, the writer can map the sequence of the different situations and corresponding pages in an array as pictured below.

A reader-response book is a challenge for bookmakers to design but a reward for book readers to enjoy again and again as they choose different options to create various space adventures.

Another activity that will stimulate the creation of a variety of books involves each student writing a story using several assigned components. Before writing begins, the teacher establishes four categories and then asks the students to generate ten items, numbered one to ten, under each category. Here is an example of part of such a chart:

	Time	Location	Climate	Central Life-form
1	2000	Earth	Hot, humid	Humans
2	3000	Moon	Frigid	Intelligent primates
3	1990	Under an ocean	No atmosphere	Vulcans
4	1999	Another galaxy	No light	Jedi Knights
5	2500	Star cruiser	Polluted	

Then students use the last four digits of their telephone numbers to select the items for their books. For instance, if the digits are 1534, a student writes a story set in the year 2000 on a star cruiser, with no outside atmosphere, and inhabited by Jedi Knights.

There are several ways of varying this writing activity. Other categories can be selected, such as hero, villain, problem, and solution. Magazine pictures depicting various settings or comic book superheroes can be used as options to excite students' imaginations. Students can pick the different items, each written on a strip of paper, from containers. Instead of a whole class activity, the teacher can organize the writing in a center for students' individual use.

Both reader-response and pick-the-components bookmaking strategies can be used for other topics. Adventures can be written about traveling back in history or living everyday life. March may come in like a dinosaur, but it leaves by transforming writing into fun and imagination for young authors.

April

Spring, Weather, and Growing

In April, signs of spring are all around us. The weather is changing, and the flowers are beginning to grow. These are all themes that young authors can use to create more stories.

SPRING

There are a variety of books that can assist students to "spring" into writing about this time of year, when nature renews itself. In *One Bright Monday Morning*, Arline and Joseph Baum use a counting pattern to list what a child observes on the way to school in spring. Aileen Fisher's *Now That Spring Is Here* poetically describes the "firsts" of spring as seen through the eyes of children. After listening to these stories, students might create their own rhyming and rhythmic verses about the joy of watching spring arrive. They could place their poems in the small blank book with butterflies and rainbows on the cover.

Writers can expand their descriptions of spring to include the other seasons. In *I Love Spring*, Clara Lewis uses a predictable pattern to describe each season. She begins with "I love (season), (Season) is (adjective)" and continues by giving examples of what the season is. She concludes each section with "That's why I love (season)." Anne Rockwell also uses a repetitive organizational style in *First Comes Spring,* in which she presents a "Bear Child" and his life through the four seasons. She describes the outdoors, his clothing, and all the familiar activities associated with each season. Both books offer predictable patterns that can be adapted easily by students to create their own stories about the seasons, the months, or holidays.

The blooming and greening of trees is an obvious characteristic of spring and a topic for books. Sharon Taylor Martin, a fellow bookmaker and teacher, created a story about trees using the rhythmic and rhyming pattern developed by Ruth Krauss in her book *Bears, bears, bears.* We adapted Sharon's idea to create a poem that describes trees from spring through winter. Challenge your students to write their own variations by sharing Krauss's book and this poem:

Trees, Trees, Trees

Sprouting leaves	Dropping leaves
Holding keys	Knocking knees
In a breeze	Drinking teas
Dressed in leaves	Without leaves
Eating peas	Copping zzzzz
Swatting bees	In a freeze

Other examples using this writing pattern include:

Flowers, flowers, flowers   or   Sun, sun, sun
Standing for hours   On the run
Enjoying showers   Always fun
Bunches in towers...   Number one...

  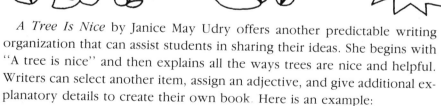

A Tree Is Nice by Janice May Udry offers another predictable writing organization that can assist students in sharing their ideas. She begins with "A tree is nice" and then explains all the ways trees are nice and helpful. Writers can select another item, assign an adjective, and give additional explanatory details to create their own book. Here is an example:

Spring vacation is fun.
Spring vacation gives you time to rest and do what you want instead of going to school and working.
Families can take special trips or visit relatives.
Spring vacation allows you more time to be outside during the daytime now that the weather is getting warmer...

Other combinations following Udry's style are also possible: "Weather is unpredictable..." or "A garden is work..." This writing pattern can assist a teacher and class to review a unit of study, such as

- adjectives in language arts — "Adjectives are descriptive."
- the brain in science — "The brain is important."
- map reading in geography — "Maps are helpful."

These books can be added to the class library for students to use as references.

WEATHER

March days are often windy, cloudy, or rainy. Help children avoid the frustrations of inclement weather by making books. To get started, read aloud *The Wind Blew* by Pat Hutchins, and encourage children to think about what happens when the wind blows. Each student can write and illustrate an idea that can be included in a class book.

Cloud Book

A book about clouds, *It Looked Like Spilt Milk* by Charles G. Shaw, provides a predictable pattern that children can use to create their own books. The illustrations are simple white cloudlike shapes on a dark blue background. The accompanying text follows a predictable pattern, telling what each shape looks like and finally explaining that the shape was really a cloud.

To create a similar book using the computer, allow the children to experiment with one of the graphic programs and input devices (see the JANUARY computer idea). Print out one shape made by each child, and ask the children to decide what their shapes resemble. On their pictures, ask them to write the text below, filling in their ideas:

I thought I saw a snake, but it wasn't a snake!
I thought I saw a ghost, but it wasn't a ghost!
I thought I saw a balloon, but it wasn't a balloon!

Compile their pictures into a book, with the last page saying:

We thought we saw all these things, but...
they were just shapes we made on the computer.

This is an easy book for inexperienced computer users to create because the pictures do not have to be perfect. They can enjoy the process of using a graphics program and creating a predictable book.

In *Hello Clouds!,* Dalia Renberg highlights how clouds can appear as different shapes and things to an imaginative child. After they listen to this book, have your students use white chalk, torn paper, or paint to create different clouds and then write text to describe what they imagine. Share Tomie de Paola's *The Cloud Book,* which humorously presents information about different clouds. Students can then create their own books on clouds, using their own observations and knowledge.

You can use the same text pattern from *It Looked Like Spilt Milk* to create books even if you don't have a computer to make the illustrations. Children can tear construction paper into shapes and decide what each one resembles. To end the text, they can write "It was just paper torn by (child's name)" in each child's book, or "They were just scraps we tore from paper" in a composite class book.

Another illustrating idea to accompany the *Spilt Milk* pattern involves the students making a series of paintings by putting tempera paint on paper and blowing the paint into patterns with straws. (Let children practice blowing paint with a straw first so they understand not to suck.) Attach their designs to, and write the text on, pages in their own blank books or one class book. Conclude their stories with "It was just paint I (we) blew through a straw."

When it rains outdoors and students are stuck in the classroom for recess, put on the silly song "Raindrops and Lemon Drops" on Joe Scruggs's album *Traffic Jams.* The children can listen and create new verses to this traditional song:

If all of the raindrops were lemon drops and gumdrops
Oh, what a wonderful world it would be.
I'd walk around with my mouth open wide.
Ahh, ahh, ahh, ahh, ahh, ahh, ahh, ahh, ahh, ahh.
If all of the raindrops were lemon drops and gumdrops
Oh, what a wonderful world it would be.

If all of the sleet were spinach and beets
Oh, what a terrible world it would be.
I'd walk around with my mouth closed tight.
Mmm, mmm, mmm, mmm, mmm, mmm, mmm, mmm, mmm, mmm.
If all of the sleet were spinach and beets
Oh, what a terrible world it would be.

Place their new verses in the small blank book with candy on the cover to create a fun songbook.

To keep the children laughing, read the silly book *Rain Makes Applesauce* by Julian Sheer. Each page presents a new absurdity and then adds "rain makes applesauce." Your students can let their imaginations run wild with words and pictures to create new books.

For more entertainment, include Judi Barrett's delightful book *Cloudy With a Chance of Meatballs.* This tall tale is about a land called "Chewand-swallow" where the food drops like rain from the sky. Each day the people's meals are described in terms of weather forecasts. The story becomes crazy when the food begins to storm. After sharing this book with your students, you can encourage the children to rewrite the school's lunch menu in meteorological language. Another possible activity would be to ask the students to describe another daily experience in different terms, such as the students' class schedule written in advertising lingo:

At 8:00 A.M. eastern time, meet your homeroom friends and teacher to hear about the day's exciting activities. You will have time to write in your journal about your special interests, secret desires, or personal concerns. At 9:00 A.M. eastern time, experience the Reading Hour. This week, join your friends to read fascinating stories about places and people from around the world...

By writing funny stories, children won't have time to wonder "whether" they are bored with the rainy "weather."

GROWING

In the spring, we become conscious of the fact that things are growing. For children, growth is not always obvious. In school, students get report cards and grades, but they may not understand what a "satisfactory" or a "B+" really means. Their bodies, as well as plants and animals, are all developing through the natural stages of life, although it may not be apparent to them in day-to-day observations. Teachers and parents can help children recognize that they, plants, and animals are growing by making books about the growth.

Raffi expresses the child's concerns about growing in his song "I Wonder If I'm Growing" on the album *Singable Songs for the Very Young.* After they listen to this song, have children brainstorm and make a book about how they have changed since fall, for instance,

height	clothes sizes	reading ability
weight	hair length	math knowledge
likes	friendships	spelling proficiency
dislikes	books read	handwriting skill

By saving their classwork and recording personal statistics from the fall, students can write about themselves by comparing fall and spring.

There are several other "growing" songs that can inspire young writers. They include:

"Everything Grows" by Raffi on his album *Everything Grows*

"Everything Grows Together" by Fred Rogers on his album *Let's Be Together Today*

"You're Growing" by Fred Rogers on his album *Won't You Be My Neighbor?*

It is important to take time in the classroom, in Sunday school, or at home to help children realize that they are changing and getting smarter, bigger, and better every day. In April, when teachers and parents may be recommending a child for retention, it is helpful to emphasize how much the child has learned and achieved during the year, even though he or she is not ready for the next grade level's demands. By making a book about her or his positive accomplishments, a child has a source of praise to be reread whenever needed.

Another sign of spring is growing plants. Let children listen to David Mallet's song about planting a garden — "Inch by Inch" recorded by Rosenshontz on their album *Tickles You!* — or to Ruth Krauss's book about planting a seed, *The Carrot Seed.* Your students can also make a book and illustrate it with photographs, drawings, and measurements recording the growth of an outside garden or simple bean seeds in cups.

Once the children have observed the life cycles of their plants, they might enjoy making a life cycle book describing the different stages of development. Using a blank-covered book, graph out the text and pictures on the right side of each double-page spread, from the first to the last page. Then flip the book upside down and backward, to start with the page closest to the back cover, and use the right side of each double-page spread in reverse. When finished, your book will become a life cycle, or "round trip," book that is read from front to back and then flipped to be read from back to front. This bookmaking strategy can also be used for adventure stories that start and end at the same place, such as a trip to school and back home for example.

Another organizational pattern for assembling a book is used in the "Turn the Wheel Books" designed by David Carter. In *How Things Grow* by Peter Seymour, the reader can turn a wheel to see pictures of five stages in the life of a cycle of a plant or animal with simple, informative text. After reading this book, encourage children to make their own books about the life cycles of other subjects by using blank books and following these steps:

A First, you will need to prepare the life cycle wheels for your book. Select seven different animals or plants to write about such as a butterfly, a frog, a flower, or a dog. 1. Cut seven circles (five-inch diameter for a small book, seven-inch diameter for a large book) out of blank stiff paper (tagboard or card stock). Divide each circle in fifths. 2. Draw the five stages of development of one life cycle in sequence on the pie-shaped parts of the circle. Be sure each drawing is placed with the center of the circle as the top of the space and the perimeter of the circle as the bottom of the space.

B Now you will need to attach the circles to the book. Prepare a template equal to a fifth of the circle. 4. Paper clip two sheets together in a blank book. 5. Place the template next to the bottom edge of the top sheet. Trace around the template and cut out an opening on the top sheet. 6. Position one life cycle circle between the paired sheets so that one fifth of the circle (one stage of the life cycle) shows through the opening. Now attach the circle to the second sheet with a paper fastener. 7. With a glue stick, attach the edges of the paired sheets together, making sure the circle can spin. Continue until all life cycle circles (wheels) are installed.

C To finish the pages of your book, add the text narrating the five stages shown on each life cycle wheel. Other variations can be made to create more stages on the wheels or more life cycle wheels in the book.

This wheel bookmaking strategy can be used to describe other sequential activities, such as directions or recipes. Other variations can be created by positioning the cut-out opening on a different spot on the page.

Finally, for another model of a life cycle book idea, see Eric Carle's *The Very Hungry Caterpillar,* which presents the life cycle of a caterpillar from egg to butterfly. Interwoven in his text is a counting book of various items that the caterpillar eats on each day of the week. The width of each page grows as the week progresses. Real holes dot the pages to look like the caterpillar truly ate the items pictured. Carle's clever bookmaking style can be used in blank books by cutting pages to various sizes and using a hole punch to create the illusion of eating.

During April, teachers can highlight spring, weather, and growing. Children and nature are all changing a little at a time. Share David Adler's *A Little at a Time* to help children see all the ways things do grow.

How to Construct a Wheel Book

1. Cut seven equal size circles out of stiff paper or card stock.

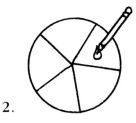

2. Divide each circle into five equal parts. Draw five stages of development for any plant or animal.

3. Cut a template out of stiff paper the size of one of the circle's five sections.

4. Paper clip two book sheets together.

5. On the first sheet of each pair, trace around the template and cut out the shape.

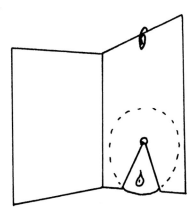

6. Position the circle between the paired sheets and attach it with a paper fastener.

7. Glue the top and outside edge of each pair of sheets. Add text to top portion of the first sheet.

   Repeat steps as often as needed.

May

Histories, Yearbooks, and Journals

In May, students can write their personal histories — things they recall from their own pasts, as well as information they gather about their parents, grandparents, and other ancestors. As the school year draws to a close, students and teachers will enjoy remembering and recording special events that have happened throughout the year. This is also the time for students to choose special stories, poems, or other writings from their creative writing journals to "publish" in a class anthology to be enjoyed over the summer. Here are some specific suggestions for these kinds of bookmaking experiences.

HISTORIES

Students look at history from a different perspective when they write about their own lives. Personal histories allow writers to research and explore their own pasts, diaries provide a means of recording the present (history in the making), and "someday" books encourage goal setting for the future.

Making personal history books gives writers a chance to talk with their parents and other relatives about their family heritage. This is the perfect time for teachers to capture their own histories in books too. Students or teachers may begin their books with drawings of their family trees, including photos of family members if available. The following questions provide guidelines for writing other pages:

Where and when was each grandparent born? (if known)

Where and when was each parent born?

What were things your parents enjoyed doing when they were your age?

What are some of the things they enjoy doing now?

What are the names and birthdays of children in the family? (Include in chronological order.)

What are the physical characteristics of each family member?

What activities does each child enjoy?

Where does the family live now?

In what other places has the family lived?

Does the family have a pet? If so, describe it.

What sports does the family enjoy?

What hobbies does the family have?

What sort of cars has the family owned?

What special trips has the family taken?

Who are special friends of the family?

Also record the family's oral history — stories frequently told in the family, but seldom written down. If these stories appear in the book, they may be saved for future generations.

While personal histories allow writers to look at their pasts, diaries help them keep an ongoing record of present events. In *Anastasia Krupnik* by Lois Lowry, a ten-year-old deals with her problems, triumphs, likes, and dislikes by making lists in a notebook. Students can use a blank book to make their own lists. Some possible list topics are Things I Like, Things I Hate, Things That Make Me Feel Proud, Things That Make Me Mad, Things That Make Me Laugh, Things That Make Me Cry, Things I Don't Understand, My Wishes, and My Favorite Places.

Brett Harvey bases the book *My Prairie Year* on a diary kept by her grandmother, who wrote down the stories of her childhood to share with Brett's mother. By writing stories from their own childhoods to share, parents or teachers may inspire students to begin keeping diaries, too. A collection of childhood memories could describe places lived, a typical school day, transportation used, daily chores, world events, and favorite holidays and pastimes.

An interesting technique for students to use when writing diaries is to include quotations from favorite books, and then write corresponding passages about experiences in real life. For instance, a quote that describes a funny predicament with a storybook dog could be followed by a funny paragraph about a real dog.

After looking back at the histories of their lives, and recording some of the events in their present lives, students can look ahead by making books that capture their dreams and hopes for the future. The predictable pattern used in Charlotte Zolotow's book *Someday* works well for this type of book. For example,

> Someday, I want to meet _____, because...
> Someday, I'd like to go to _____, because...
> Someday, I want to learn more about _____, because...
> Someday, my house will be...
> Someday, I'd like to be a...
> Someday, I want to spend more time...
> Someday, I hope...
> Someday, I want to write a book about...

YEARBOOKS

Another way to record memories is to make a book that recalls one year of life. *Through the Year with Harriet,* by Betsy and Giulio Maestro, gives a month-by-month account of one year in Harriet's life. Students can illustrate a book describing some of their activities during the year by using their own drawings or other artwork saved from each month and pictures from a calendar. Alternatively, students could write and illustrate two pages of a blank book each month during the school year. With school-wide cooperation or in a home setting, a similar book could be made, with two pages added each year from kindergarten through graduation.

A different style of yearbook might be organized by topic rather than by month. Some topics that could be included are

> Favorite books I've read
> The most special books I've made
> Favorite songs
> Important class projects
> Special people who visited our classroom
> Places we've gone (field trips)
> People in my class (autograph pages)

Index tabs could be used to help organize the book (see the DECEMBER compter idea).

Before students sign their classmates' autograph pages, they may enjoy reading or hearing some excerpts from *Yours Till Niagara Falls,* compiled by Lillian Morrison. The book is an anthology of poems and jokes traditionally used in autograph books. Give children some time to make up a poem or a joke they would like to include in their classmates' books.

Teachers who create a yearbook of classroom activities will have a preview to share with the next year's parents and students, as well as a record of some of their favorite curriculum ideas. The pages for each month might contain pictures and written descriptions of bulletin boards used, field trips taken, books created, and special projects completed.

In Maurice Sendak's *Chicken Soup With Rice,* the main character takes the reader through each month with a "chicken soup" theme. Changing the theme, this strategy can be used to highlight other subjects — like bookmaking!

In January I'll want to share
books I write about my teddy bear.
Writing here,
Writing there,
Making books beyond compare.

In February I'll design
a book about a valentine.
Designing here,
Designing there,
Making books beyond compare.

In March I'll draw an alien's face
to decorate my book on space.
Drawing here,
Drawing there,
Making books beyond compare.

Continue this pattern for each month of the year. Illustrate with children's artwork or photos of the books made. Then end with:

I've said it here,
I've said it there.
Every month with great care
I've made a book beyond compare.

JOURNALS

Creative writing journals give young authors an opportunity to write every day. For ideas on scheduling this activity, see chapter 4. By rehearsing their writing and drawing in the journals, students can refine and edit their ideas in second and third drafts for possible bookmaking.

There are many sources of ideas for creative writing topics. These ideas should be presented as suggestions for journal writing — not as assignments. Allow enough flexibility that students can choose their own topics, but also provide writing suggestions as a catalyst for the students who need help getting started.

One strategy involves taking components from a basal story and weaving them into the plot of a new story, as Lolly, Spider, and Sam do in *Three by the Sea* by Edward Marshall. Lolly first reads a dull story about a cat and a rat. Sam and Spider then each tell more exciting stories of a cat and a rat. Challenge students to take characters, settings, or plots from basal stories and change them to make a new tale.

Imagine That! by Joyce Strauss provides page after page of questions to stimulate imagination. Each question could be the topic for a journal entry. At the end of the book, readers are invited to create more questions of their own. Pages from the book could be removed and laminated to serve as task cards at a writing center. Students can create additional task cards by making up new situations. For example,

Imagine you find a magic coin that can take you any place in the world. How and where did you find it? Where will you have the coin take you?

Pretend you and your dog exchange bodies for the day. What experiences will each of you have?

Imagine you can fly. Where will you go? What things will you see?

Margaret Wise Brown's *The Important Book* uses a predictable pattern students could adopt for their journals. Students might choose to alter the pattern to describe what was best or special about something. For example,

The best part of a cake is the icing.
The cake itself tastes delicious,
and the candy decorations are beautiful,
but the best part of a cake is the icing.

The best part of the school day is recess.
I like to sing in music class,
and go to the school library for new books,
but the best part of the school day is recess.

Inspiration for creative writing may also come from Charlotte Zolotow's *Do You Know What I'll Do?*, which tells the story of a little girl promising her brother the things she'll do for him. The text is a repeating pattern of questions and answers. Help your students explore different questions to ask and ways to respond. For example,

Can you guess what I'd say if there were just one cookie left?
"You can have the biggest half."

Can you guess what I'd say if you were scared of a thunderstorm?
"You can sleep in my bed tonight."

Continue the pattern, and finish with a question that will create an ending, such as,

Can you guess what I'd say when I finished reading you a story?
"I'll read you another one tomorrow."

After students have written in their journals, allow time during the week's schedule for them to share their ideas with you and their peers. As presented in chapter 2, students should receive feedback on the content of their work rather than on its form. After they refine their texts, they can edit their work to follow language conventions (correct spelling and punctuation, proper grammar, and clear, legible handwriting). In May, teachers can ask students to select favorite drawings and pieces of writing from their journals to revise and edit for placement in a class or personal anthology. Once editing is complete, the computer can be used as a tool to help publish the writing.

Publishing a Journal Anthology

Computer Idea

Computer programs chosen to assist in publication of a journal anthology will depend on the skill level of your students, as well as software, peripherals, and amount of time available. Because printing requirements will vary widely, it is important to make sure that whatever package you select will work with your printer. Check the manual or the outside of the software package to determine compatibility with your printer. Printing out a sample copy before using the software with children can avoid frustration later.

Students operating at a very basic level could use software like *Kidwriter Gold*™ by Spinnaker or a program from Pelican® Software's *Creating Writing Series*. These programs include pre-made backgrounds and objects that students can select to create illustrations and simple word processors for entering text.

Using *Kidwriter Gold*, children are able to see their pictures as they write their stories. When printed, graphics appear at the top of a sheet of paper, and the text on the bottom. No change in the size of illustrations or the layout of text is possible.

In programs from the *Creative Writing Series*, pictures must be created first and saved or printed before the story is written. The author is unable to view his or her picture on the monitor while writing the story, but several different options for layout and size are available when printing text and graphics.

Springboard's *The Newsroom*^{TM} and LCSI's *LogoWriter*^{TM} require additional time and skill to learn and use, but allow more sophisticated integration of text and graphics. Be sure to spend sufficient time with these programs yourself before introducing them to your students so you will be able to answer the technical questions that are sure to arise.

Another way to "publish" the journal anthology is to use an easy but full-featured word processor such as Multiscribe™ by StyleWare. *Picture Manager*^{TM} (available separately) allows you to add computer graphics to *Multiscribe* documents. Enough copies can be printed out for all students, or one set can be printed and the rest photocopied.

Another alternative is for students to hand-illustrate pages after they are printed. If only the text appears on each page, one student can read his or her contribution aloud as classmates each draw a picture on their own copies of that page. This helps check comprehension, since students must have an understanding of what was read in order to illustrate the passage.

Once pages have been printed out and reproduced, they can be mounted in blank books so each student will have a copy of the anthology to take home. Extra copies could be prepared for the school library, the principal, classroom volunteers, etc.

Personal histories, yearbooks, and journal anthologies close the school year by helping writers first recall, then record, and later look back and remember some of the special times in their lives. In years to come, these books will remind them about what they did and things they thought about during their elementary school years. In addition, the books are sure to be popular at future class reunions or teacher retirement teas.

# Summer

"Reading Rainbow,"
Summer Fun, and Potpourri

Summer is the time for recreational reading and writing. Whether a student is in summer school for remediation, or in camp for enrichment, the emphasis of instruction should be on integrating reading and writing and making that process enjoyable. Summer activities, such as watching "Reading Rainbow," going on picnics, or calling friends, can provide ideas for creating books.

"READING RAINBOW"

"Reading Rainbow" is the summer's hottest PBS television program for children. Each thirty-minute episode of the series is introduced with a television adaptation of a picture book appropriate for beginning readers. Specific themes from the books are expanded to other situations to motivate children to make reading a part of their everyday lives. The series can also be used to encourage students to make writing part of their daily experiences. By focusing on selected "Reading Rainbow" books, children can experiment with writing different genres, such as tall tales, folktales, myths, and fairy tales.

Tall Tales

After listening to the tall tale *Paul Bunyan* by Steven Kellogg, ask your students to brainstorm all the exaggerations about Paul and the explanations of nature associated with him. Then map out the plot with them to determine the format of a tall tale that they can use as a pattern to design their own stories. For more ideas about the language and story development of a tall tale, assign students to read:

- other descriptions of Paul Bunyan, such as *Ol' Paul The Mighty Logger* by Glen Rounds

- other tall tales about legendary heroes, such as *Pecos Bill* retold by Steven Kellogg

- silly tales, such as Sid Fleischman's *McBroom Tells a Lie*

Students will enjoy creating a funny tale about a new folk hero who has outlandish abilities or catastrophies.

Folktales and Myths

"Reading Rainbow" also presents special folktales that offer writing patterns for young authors to use. In the African tale *Bringing the Rain to Kapiti Plain*, Verna Aardema poetically retells an old tale from the Nandi tribe, using the style of the cumulative nursery rhyme, "The House That Jack Built." Young authors can use this pattern to create a story:

This is a boy who is going to school.

This is the bus, all yellow and bright,
that picked up the boy who's off to school.

This is the teacher, standing by the door,
who met the bus, all yellow and bright,
that picked up the boy who's off to school.

Another book that can be used to demonstrate this writing style is *This Is the Bear* by Sarah Hayes, in which a bear takes a trip to the garbage dump. Children can have fun relating their experiences using this writing style.

Students can also write about folktales that explain nature. In another "Reading Rainbow" book, *The Gift of the Sacred Dog*, Paul Goble describes how the Great Spirit rewards a determined Indian boy with the first horses, Sacred Dogs, for the boy's tribe. Students can retell other myths that describe the origins of different animals to create their own books. To get the students started, ask them to follow the writing pattern used in the story:

1. Describe the people and their situation without the animal selected, and be sure to create a need in their lives for the animal.

2. Set up a way for the god to give the animal to a person, and provide the god's explanation of the gift.

3. Conclude with the person returning to share with his or her new animals with the other people.

Stories can be written explaining nature's creation. The Greek myths provide other written examples. As explained in Chapter 1, it is helpful to offer students a pattern for writing.

Fairy Tales

Various versions of fairy tales are available for children to read and analyze. In the prologue of the "Reading Rainbow" book *Rumpelstiltskin*, Paul Zelinsky explains how he compiled the text for his story by combining elements from different accounts of this tale. Children can create their own versions of fairy tales by combining elements of different versions about Snow White, Rapunzel, or Jack and the Beanstalk.

Students can also consider these other possibilities for writing original adaptations of fairy tales:

1. Combine elements of different fairy tales to create a new tale.

2. Write yourself into a fairy tale. How could you help the hero or heroine escape the villain to create a happy ending?

3. Modernize the fairy tale to the twentieth century.

If you like these creative writing ideas based on "Reading Rainbow" books, check the previous months' ideas for additional examples:

SEPTEMBER — Field Trips	*The Day Jimmy's Boa Ate the Wash* by Trinka Hakes Noble
NOVEMBER — Friends	*We Are Best Friends* by Aliki
JANUARY — Habitats	*Gila monsters meet you at the airport* by Marjorie Weinman Sharmat
MARCH — Past	*Digging Up Dinosaurs* by Aliki
MARCH — Present	*Imogene's Antlers* by David Small
MAY — Journals	*Three by the Sea* by Edward Marshall
SUMMER — Summer Fun	*Three Days on a River in a Red Canoe* by Vera Williams

SUMMER FUN

During the summertime, families may have extra time available to experiment with artwork, go on picnics, and take trips. Each of these enjoyable experiences can be a rich source of ideas for bookmaking.

Art Ideas

Many of our bookmaking suggestions have begun with ways to write the text for a book, and then use illustrations to support the text. Children may reverse the process by creating pictures to tell a story, then adding some accompanying text if desired. Here are some techniques to create artwork that could become the basis for special picture books:

Gadget Painting   A student dips a cookie cutter, a spool, a potato masher, or another gadget into a shallow pan of liquid tempera paint, then presses it on paper. This process is especially good for creating counting books because it makes it easy to get many identical images.

Rain Painting   Children sprinkle dry tempera paint in a variety of colors on pieces of paper and place the papers outside. Raindrops make interesting patterns appear on the papers. Children can add line drawings to the patterned background, then write stories to go along with the pictures they create.

Thumbprint Drawing   Students like transforming fingerprints into animals, people, or objects. With some inspiration from *Fingerprint Owls and Other Fantasies* by Marjorie Katz or Ed Emberley's *Great Thumbprint Drawing Book,* fingerprint worlds will soon decorate the pages of their "handmade" picture books.

Straw Painting   Students drip tempera paint onto paper, then with a straw, blow the paint gently in different directions. Details can be added to the pictures with paintbrushes, markers, crayons, or torn paper.

Protect paintings and thumbprint pictures by spraying them with clear acrylic spray before they are mounted in blank books, or covering the pictures with clear self-adhesive plastic after they are pasted in the books.

Picnics

Picnics are a great part of summer fun! *The Great Race* by Stephen Wyllie and Anni Axworthy tells an exciting tale of animals on their way to a picnic. A unique feature of this book is that it includes color-coded cutouts of characters, places, and food, to be inserted in slots throughout the book, so a reader can change the story. To make a book of this style with interchangeable characters, children can create their own cutouts and use a repositionable adhesive, such as Dennison's "Tack a Note"™ stick or 3-M's "Post-it™ tape, to make the pictures self-sticking and removable. Young authors can then write a first draft of their text on scratch paper. After editing, the text is copied into a blank book, leaving spaces between words for the cutouts to be attached when the book is read. An envelope could be pasted to the inside back cover to hold the cutout pieces when they are not in use.

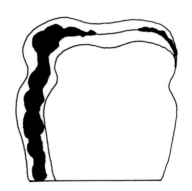

A picnic-basket book with the inside pages cut to resemble food shapes.

Picnic songs can inspire books, too. Listen to Raffi singing Lynn Olson's song "Going on a Picnic," on the album *The Corner Grocery Store*, or Sharon, Lois, and Bram singing "On a Picnic We Will Go," on the album *Elephant Show Record*. Both songs involve repeating patterns of questions about what items were brought for a picnic. To make a picnic songbook, students can create their own questions about items packed to take along on a picnic. Position a blank book so that it opens with the binding on the bottom. Attach posterboard picnic baskets with handles to the front and back outside covers. Inside pages can be cut into food shapes. For example, use an apple-shaped page with the following text:

Have you packed some apples, apples, apples?
Yes, I've packed some apples just for you!

Trips

Families often take advantage of summer vacations by going on trips. Those special times can be relived if books are created to preserve the memories. Combine children's drawings of what they've seen, photographs of places visited, pictures from brochures, and postcards of favorite sights to illustrate a book about the trip. Older children can write the accompanying story themselves, while younger children may be more comfortable dictating a text to an adult or an older sibling. Adults will enjoy contributing to the text, too! A rough draft of each page can be written on scratch paper or self-sticking repositionable memo paper. Once the authors are happy with the text, it can be transferred to the pages of a blank book, and illustrations added. The "Reading Rainbow" episode that features Vera Williams's book *Three Days on a River in a Red Canoe* gives an excellent demonstration of children creating a book about their trip.

An ingenious book by Vera and Jennifer Williams, *Stringbean's Trip to the Shining Sea,* describes two brothers' vacation through the picture postcards they send to their family. Interspersed with the postcards are album pages containing photos taken during the trip. To create their own postcard book about a trip, young authors have two choices. They may use ready-made postcards collected from a trip (or sent by traveling relatives), or they can make their own picture postcards. Plan text for the book in such a way that the writing on each picture postcard adds something to the story sequence.

Sooner or later, the question of appropriate behavior during summer travels will come up. Elizabeth Bridgman's *How to Travel with Grownups* explains trip etiquette in a way that will make both adults and children laugh. While the text gives suggestions of proper behavior, the pictures show mischievous children breaking each rule. Children can make a parallel "How to Travel with Children" guide for adults. To get started, have them think of suggestions they might give to parents during traveling. They can then write a text that follows those suggestions, but draw illustrations that show adults acting in a way that contradicts the text.

Summer trips provide wonderful opportunities for language and word play, regardless of whether children are traveling miles with their families, or to the local museum or zoo with parents or teachers. "I'm going on a trip" is a familiar word game that can first be played in the car, then used as the basis for making a book. The traditional version goes like this:

First player: I'm going on a trip, and I'm going to take an *apple* (or any object that begins with the letter *a*).

Second player: I'm going on a trip, and I'm going to take an *apple* and a *baseball.*

Third player: I'm going on a trip, and I'm going to take an *apple,* a *banana,* and a *canoe.*

Each player repeats the objects being taken and adds a new object that starts with the next letter of the alphabet.

The game can also be played by organizing the series of objects by numbers or categories instead of in alphabetical sequence. Here is a sample of a game combining numbers and a category (zoo):

First player: I went to the zoo, and I saw *one kangaroo.*

Second player: I went to the zoo, and I saw *one kangaroo* and *two zebras.*

Third player: I went to the zoo, and I saw *one kangaroo, two zebras,* and *three monkeys.*

With the help of the computer, children can make a counting book based on this game.

Computer Idea

Counting Book

To make the pages for this book, use a program like *Stickybear Printer*™ or *SuperPrint!*™ which allow small graphics to be repeated any number of times and placed in any position on a background scene.

Follow the game format during the creation of the book by allowing each student to do one page of graphics and text. For example, the first student might choose an outdoor background and a barn for graphics, and write:

> I went to *the farm,*
> and I saw one red *barn.*

This page is printed out, or saved to be printed later. The second student uses the graphics created by the first student, then adds two more objects:

> I went to *the farm,*
> and I saw one red *barn* and two big *cats.*

The third student continues in the same way, with the number in the second line increasing until the last number of desired objects is reached. Teachers may wish to divide their classes into two or three groups, each working on a different theme.

Because the "full page" design of *Stickybear Printer* actually fills only half of an 8½ " x 11 " page, you may want to have students design the graphics first when using this program. The picture can then be printed on the top half of the page, and the text can be entered separately to be printed on the bottom half of the same page. Another alternative is to mount graphics only in the blank book and cover each page with clear self-adhesive plastic. Children can write their text with a washable overhead marking pen, then wipe it off so the next reader can also write a text for the picture story.

POTPOURRI

Summer is the perfect time for children to experiment with books that provide special kinds of information and books that will use fun language patterns.

Books can be very useful for retrieving all sorts of information, including phone numbers, instructions, or word meanings.

Phone Books   A blank book can be used to create a personal phone book. Emergency numbers, parents' work numbers, friends' and relatives' numbers can all be included, with a picture to accompany each.

Instructional Books   A favorite hobby or activity can become the inspiration for a how-to book. Perhaps you know a child who could write one of these books: *How to Catch a Fish, How to Weave a Pot Holder, How to Care for a Hermit Crab,* or *How to Get in Trouble.*

Dictionaries   Dictionaries are an important source of information, and one made by students can be very special because it contains the words that are most important to them. Use two large blank books to create a two-volume classroom picture dictionary. The first volume includes letters *A-M,* and the second volume, letters *N-Z.* This division allows a double-page spread for each letter, leaving room for a title page in each volume. Students can cut colorful alphabet letters from construction or fadeless art paper, decorate, and place in appropriate positions in the book. When a student wonders how a word is spelled, the first step is to look in the regular dictionary or ask a classmate or the teacher. Once the correct spelling of a word is determined, the student enters that word in the appropriate place in the classroom dictionary with a small illustration. A sentence using the word in context may be written as well. Spelling words and science and social studies vocabulary words can also be included.

Taking a closer look at dictionaries may generate interest in word origins. *Where Words Were Born* by Arkady Leokum, Paul Posnick, and Stanley Corwin gives the history of more than one hundred common words. *Guppies and Tuxedos* by Marvin Terban tells the origins of words that were derived from the names of people and places. For instance, candy was named after Prince Charles de Conde, who loved sweets. Encourage students to research where a variety of words came from to make their own book of etymology.

Language Fun Books

Books can be made to highlight language fun using word meanings and associations, analogies, antonyms, idioms, homonyms, or codes. Try using the following published books as springboards for creative writing ideas.

Word Meanings and Associations *What's in a Word?* by Rosalie Moscovitch takes a lighthearted look at word definitions. For example, the definition of the word *erasing* shows a picture of an *E* in a foot race. The back of the book gives the real definitions for each word featured.

Ruth Krauss presents a book of definitions using a predictable sentence pattern in *A Hole is to Dig*. Children can generate their own definitions of words to form the text for a book, such as:

Umbrellas are to keep you dry when it rains.
Hands are to cover your mouth when you cough.
Stories are to read when it's time for bed.

Purple is Part of a Rainbow by Carolyn Kowalczyk provides another pattern for word association. Students can take an item and explain what it is a part of, for instance,

A house is part of a neighborhood.
Bones are part of a body.
A cloud is a part of the sky.

For more capable students, Judi Barrett offers a funny way to present descriptive associations in *A Snake is Totally Tail*. She develops a writing pattern by naming an animal and then describing an attribute through the use of alliteration. Students' variations might look something like this:

A dog is forever friendly.
A cat is cautiously caring.
A monkey is mostly mischievous.

Other fun with word combinations is offered by Charlotte Zolotow's book *Some Things Go Together*, Judi Barrett's book *Pickles Have Pimples and Other Silly Statements*, and Hap Palmer's song, "They Go Together" on the album *Witches' Brew*. Teachers can share examples from these sources with their students and challenge them to create more combinations, such as:

- blankets on beds and hats on heads
- sandwiches with chips and vegetables with dips
- reading with books and food with cooks

Analogies The book *Easy as Pie* by Marcia and Michael Folsom presents familiar analogies in an alphabet guessing game format. Brainstorm with students to write additional familiar or invented sayings in the following riddle style:

A...red as an
Apple

B...busy as a
Bee

C...quiet as a
Cat

Antonyms   Word play can be fun for children from the earliest age with books that portray opposites. One page may picture an empty crate with the word *Empty* written beneath it while the facing page shows the same crate filled with toys, with the word *Full* below it. See Tana Hoban's book of photographs, *Push, Pull, Empty, Full,* for additional examples. Children can draw and label pictures of opposites, or they can cut illustrations that demonstrate antonyms from magazines. Then each child can contribute a pair of pictures to be assembled in a blank book about opposites.

More capable students may enjoy the challenge of using pictures with flaps to depict each antonyms, as Eric Hill does in his book *Opposites.* In one picture, a child might draw a picnic table with an empty basket on it. The question on the page might read, "What is the opposite of empty?" A flap shaped as a tablecloth could be lifted to show a full picnic basket underneath with the label, "full."

Idioms   Two books by Fred Gwynne, *The King Who Rained* and *A Chocolate Moose for Dinner,* take a humorous approach to idioms by illustrating their literal meanings. Children will enjoy making a book of this style. Brainstorm for a variety of sayings similar to the ones Fred Gwynne uses. Some possibilities are:

> Text: The word is right on the tip of my tongue.
> Picture: Tongue with a word written on its tip.

> Text: It's raining cats and dogs.
> Picture: Cats and dogs falling from the sky.

> Text: She put her foot in her mouth.
> Picture: Girl with her foot in her mouth.

Riddle Romp by Giulio Maestro and *What's Your Name?* by Scott Peterson explore idioms in a riddle format. After reading these books, challenge your students to each create a page to include in a classroom riddle book. For example,

> Q: Why did the nervous scientist go get a net?
> A: He wanted to catch the butterflies in his stomach.

Homonyms   More word play riddles can be found in two books by Guilio Maestro that look at different types of homonyms. The riddles in *What's a Frank Frank?* are homographs, which are words that are spelled the same but have different meanings. *What's Mite Might?* uses homophones, which are words that sound the same but are spelled differently and have different meanings. Ask your students to write and illustrate some riddles of both types in a blank book. For a book of homographs, a child might write:

Q: Why did Sally find a fork in the fork?
A: She dropped her silverware at the place where the road divided.

A riddle for a book of homophones might read:

Q: When do you hear what is here?
A: When you are listening in this place.

Code   For fun with letters written as a code, *C C D B!* by William Steig. F U R not E-Z 2 fool, U L B OK with this book. School authors can all have fun trying their skill at writing this type of code, then assembling the results in a blank book with cute illustrations.

A clever book that also uses a code as part of its text is *The Secret Birthday Message* by Eric Carle. A boy receives a secret message on his birthday, and must crack the code to find his present. Pages are cut in shapes of clues in the message, such as a moon, a star, and stair steps. This book can be used as inspiration for students to write their own book with a secret message, or simply as an example that pages don't always have to be square when making a book.

By making books about favorite "Reading Rainbow" episodes, summer fun, language and word play, and books of special use to them, children learn that words can go together to entertain or inform.

Appendix

Checklist for a Young Authors' Conference

1. Form a committee of teachers, parents, and possibly students to brainstorm the variety of activities to be included in the young authors' program. You may want to schedule
   - a kickoff event to start the bookwriting, such as a teachers' inservice, a parent education night, or a student assembly to suggest bookmaking ideas and procedures:
   - a series of sessions at which students can receive help editing and publishing their books;
   - the culminating young authors' conference, at which teachers, parents, and children can read and display books written.
2. Check calendar to secure dates and available locations. Be sure to schedule around other extracurricular activities, such as sports competitions or science fairs. You may want to investigate guest speakers for the kickoff event and/or young authors' conference.
3. Prepare a budget for your young authors' program. Include the costs of any bookmaking supplies that will be provided to students and any awards to be given to the conference participants. You may want to secure financial underwriting for the activities and materials selected. Parent-teacher organizations, the school system, a local reading group (International Reading Association), or private businesses can provide the needed monetary support.
4. Formally prepare the program schedule, and finalize any contractual agreements regarding meeting locations and speaker reservations. Order bookmaking supplies and any awards for the participants in the conference. Reserve any special equipment needed. Notify the press or school newsletter of your program to arrange coverage of the different activities.
5. Recruit volunteers to help children in the classroom with publishing their books and to host the various events planned. They may help decorate the conference site, prepare a program brochure, and serve refreshments.
6. Promote participation of all children, parents, and teachers in all phases of the conference.

This unique book
was created by

_____

on _____

Be Enthusiastic About Reading
Create Unique Books

**Be
Enthusiastic
About
Reading

Create
Unique
Books**

This unique book
was created by
_____
especially for
_____
_____

on _____

YOUNG AUTHOR'S AWARD

This certifies that

_____

merits this special writer's award.

Presented by _____

This ____ day of _____ , 19 ___

Bibliography

REFERENCES

Harste, Jerome, and Kathy Short, with Carolyn Burke. *Creating Classrooms for Authors.* Portsmouth, N.H.: Heinemann, 1988.

Irvine, Joan. *How to Make Pop-Ups.* New York: Morrow Junior Books, 1987.

Johnston, Lynn. *It Must Be Nice to Be Little.* Kansas City: Andrews and McMeel, 1983.

Lamme, Linda. *Growing Up Writing.* Washington, D.C.: Acropolis Books, 1984.

Larrick, Nancy. *A Parent's Guide to Children's Reading.* 4th ed. New York: Bantam Books, 1975.

Moss, Joy. *Focus Units in Literature: A Handbook for Elementary School Teachers.* Urbanna, Ill.: National Council of Teachers of English, 1984.

Roser, Nancy, and Margaret Firth, eds. *Children's Choices: Teaching with Books Children Like.* Newark, Del.: International Reading Association, 1983.

Trelease, Jim. *The Read-Aloud Handbook.* New York: Penguin Books, 1979.

CHILDREN'S BOOKS

Aardema, Verna. *Bringing the Rain to Kapiti Plain.* Dial Books, 1981. (SUMMER — "Reading Rainbow")

A Book of Ghosts. Child's Play, 1974. (OCTOBER — Fall)

Adams, Pam. *If I weren't for me...who would I be?* Child's Play, 1981. (NOVEMBER — Careers)

Adler, David. *A Little at a Time.* Random House, 1976. (APRIL — Growing)

Adler, David. *The Twisted Witch and Other Spooky Riddles.* Holiday House, 1985. (OCTOBER — Riddles)

Ahlberg, Janet and Allan. *The Jolly Postman or Other People's Letters.* Little, Brown, 1986. (FEBRUARY — Valentine's Day)

Aliki. *Digging Up Dinosaurs.* Harper & Row, 1981. (MARCH — Past)

Aliki. *How a Book is Made.* Thomas Y. Crowell, 1986. (Chapter 4)

Aliki. *We Are Best Friends.* Mulberry Books, 1982. (NOVEMBER — Friends)

Ames, Lee. *Draw 50 Famous Faces.* Doubleday, 1978. (FEBRUARY — Presidents' Day)

Asch, Frank. *Just Like Daddy.* Simon & Schuster, 1981. (NOVEMBER — Family)

Back, Christine, and Barrie Watts. *Spider's Web*. Silver
    Burdett, 1984. (Chapter 2, JANUARY — Animals)
Balian, Lorna. *The Humbug Witch*. Abingdon, 1965.
    (OCTOBER — Halloween)
Barrett, Judi. *Animals should definitely not act like people*.
    Atheneum, 1980. (JANUARY — Animals)
Barrett, Judi. *Animals should definitely not wear clothing*.
    Atheneum, 1970. (Chapters 1 & 2, JANUARY — Animals)
Barrett, Judi. *A Snake is Totally Tail*. Aladdin Books,
    1983. (SUMMER — Potpourri)
Barrett, Judi. *Cloudy With a Chance of Meatballs*. Atheneum,
    1979. (Chapters 1 & 2, APRIL — Weather)
Barrett, Judi. *Pickles Have Pimples and Other Silly Statements*.
    Atheneum, 1986. (Chapter 2, SUMMER — Potpourri)
Barth, Edna. *Holly, Reindeer, and Colored Lights*. Clarion,
    1971. (DECEMBER — Traditions)
Barth, Edna. *Witches, Pumpkins, and Grinning Ghosts*.
    Clarion, 1972. (OCTOBER — Fall)
Baum, Arline and Joseph. *One Bright Monday Morning*. Random
    House, 1962. (APRIL — Spring)
Berenstain, Stan and Jan. *The Berenstain Bears Get Stage Fright*.
    Random House, 1986. (NOVEMBER — Family)
Berenstain, Stan and Jan. *The Berenstain Bears Visit the Dentist*.
    Random House, 1981. (NOVEMBER — Family)
Berenstain, Stan and Jan. *The Bike Lesson*. Random House, 1968.
    (FEBRUARY — Valentine's Day)
Blume, Judy. *The Pain and The Great One*. Bradbury Press, 1974.
    (NOVEMBER — Family)
Bond, Michael. *A Bear Called Paddington*. Dell, 1968.
    (FEBRUARY — Valentine's Day)
Brandenberg, Franz. *A Secret for Grandmother's Birthday*.
    Greenwillow Books, 1975. (DECEMBER — Gifts)
Broekel, Ray. *I Can Be an Author*. Children's Press, 1986.
    (Chapter 4)
Bridgman, Elizabeth. *How to Travel with Grownups*. Thomas Y.
    Crowell, 1980. (SUMMER — Summer Fun)
Bright, Robert. *Georgie's Halloween*. Doubleday, 1958
    (OCTOBER — Halloween)
Brown, Jeff. *Flat Stanley*. Scholastic, 1972. (MARCH — Present)
Brown, Margaret Wise. *The Important Book*. Harper & Row, 1949.
    (MAY — Journals)
Burningham, John. *Would You Rather...*Thomas Y. Crowell, 1978.
    (JANUARY — Habitats)
Burns, Diane L. *Elephants Never Forget!* Lerner Publications,
    1987. (JANUARY — Animals)
Campbell, Rod. *Dear Zoo*. Four Winds Press, 1982. (JANUARY —
    Animals)

Carle, Eric. *The Secret Birthday Message.* Harper & Row,
1972. (Chapter 2, SUMMER — Potpourri)

Carle, Eric. *The Very Busy Spider.* Philomel, 1985.
(Chapter 2, JANUARY — Animals)

Carle, Eric. *The Very Hungry Caterpillar.* Scholastic, 1970.
(Chapter 2, APRIL — Growing)

Cerf, Bennett. *Book of Animal Riddles.* Beginner Books,
1964. (JANUARY — Animals)

Chaikin, Miriam. *Light Another Candle: The Story and Meaning
of Hanukkah.* Clarion, 1981. (DECEMBER — Traditions)

Charlip, Remy. *Fortunately.* Parents, 1964. (MARCH — Present)

Cleary, Beverly. *Ramona the Pest.* Dell, 1968. (Chapters 1 & 2,
NOVEMBER — Family, MARCH — Present)

Cole, Joanna. *The Magic School Bus: At the Waterworks.*
Scholastic, 1986. (SEPTEMBER — Field Trips)

Cole, Joanna. *The Magic School Bus: Inside the Earth.*
Scholastic, 1987. (SEPTEMBER — Field Trips)

Craig, M. Jean. *Dinosaurs and More Dinosaurs.* Scholastic,
1965. (MARCH — Past)

de Paola, Tomie. *The Cloud Book.* Holiday House, 1975.
(APRIL — Weather)

Edelman, Elaine. *I Love My Baby Sister (Most of the Time).*
Puffin, 1984. (NOVEMBER — Family)

Elting, Mary, and Michael Folsom. *Q is for Duck.* Houghton
Mifflin/Clarion, 1980. (SEPTEMBER — School Routines)

Emberley, Ed. *Drawing Book of Animals.* Little, Brown, 1970.
(JANUARY — Animals)

Emberley, Ed. *Great Thumbprint Drawing Book.* Little,
Brown, 1977. (SUMMER — Summer Fun)

Emberley, Ed. *Make a World: A Drawing Book.* Little, Brown,
1972. (Chapter 3)

Emberley, Michael. *Dinosaurs!* Little, Brown, 1980. (MARCH — Past)

Fisher, Aileen. *Now That Spring Is Here,* Bowmar, 1977. (APRIL — Spring)

Fleischman, Sid. *McBroom Tells a Lie.* Little, Brown, 1976.
(SUMMER — ''Reading Rainbow'')

Folsom, Marcia and Michael. *Easy as Pie.* Clarion, 1985.
(SUMMER — Potpourri, OCTOBER — Riddles)

Freeman, Don. *Corduroy.* Viking Press, 1968. (FEBRUARY —
Valentine's Day)

Giff, Patricia Reilly. *Today Was a Terrible Day.* Puffin,
1980. (Chapter 2, MARCH — Present)

Goble, Paul. *The Gift of the Sacred Dog.* Bradbury Press, 1980.
(SUMMER — ''Reading Rainbow'')

Gwynne, Fred. *A Chocolate Moose for Dinner.* Prentice Hall, 1976.
(SUMMER — Potpourri)

Gwynne, Fred. *The King Who Rained.* Prentice Hall, 1970
(SUMMER — Potpourri)

Hallinan, P.K. *That's What a Friend Is*. Children's Press, 1977. (NOVEMBER — Friends)

Harvey, Brett. *My Prairie Year*. Holiday House, 1986. (MAY — Histories)

Hayes, Sarah. *This Is the Bear*. Harper & Row, 1986. (SUMMER — "Reading Rainbow")

Heide, Florence. *Shrinking Treehorn*. Holiday House, 1971. (MARCH — Present)

Hill, Eric. *Nursery Rhyme PEEK-A-BOOK*. Price/Sloan/Stern, 1982. (OCTOBER — Riddles)

Hill, Eric. *Opposites*. Price/Sloan/Stern, 1982. (SUMMER — Potpourri)

Hoban, Tana. *Push, Pull, Empty, Full*. Macmillan, 1972. (SUMMER — Potpourri)

Hoberman, Mary Ann. *A House Is a House for Me*. Puffin Books, 1978. (JANUARY — Habitats)

Hutchins, Pat. *The Wind Blew*. Macmillan, 1974. (APRIL — Weather)

Irvine, Joan. *How to Make Pop-Ups*. Morrow Junior Books, 1987. (Chapter 3, JANUARY — Animals)

I thought I saw. Child's Play, 1974. (OCTOBER — Fall)

Jackson, Kathryn. *The Joys of Christmas*. Golden Press, 1976. (DECEMBER — Traditions)

Joslin, Sesyle. *What Do You Do, Dear?* Harper & Row, 1961. (SEPTEMBER — School Routines)

Joslin, Sesyle. *What Do You Say, Dear?* Harper & Row, 1958. (SEPTEMBER — School Routines)

Katz, Marjorie. *Fingerprint Owls and Other Fantasies*. M. Evans, 1972. (SUMMER — Summer Fun)

Kellogg, Steven. *Paul Bunyan*. Morrow, 1984. (SUMMER — "Reading Rainbow")

Kellogg, Steven. *Pecos Bill*. Morrow, 1986. (SUMMER — "Reading Rainbow")

Kowalczyk, Carolyn. *Purple Is Part of a Rainbow*. Children's Press, 1985. (SUMMER — Potpourri)

Krauss, Ruth. *A Hole Is to Dig*. Harper & Row, 1952. (SUMMER — Potpourri)

Krauss, Ruth. *Bears, bears, bears*. Scholastic, 1948. (APRIL — Spring)

Krauss, Ruth. *The Carrot Seed*. Scholastic, 1945. (APRIL — Growing)

Kroll, Steven. *The Tyrannosaurus Game*. Holiday House, 1976. (MARCH — Past)

Lasky, Kathryn. *I Have Four Names for My Grandfather*. Little, Brown, 1976. (Chapter 1, NOVEMBER — Family)

Leokum, Arkady, Paul Posnick, and Stanley Corwin. *Where Words Were Born*. Corwin Books, 1977. (SUMMER — Potpourri)

Lewis, Clara. *I Love Spring.* Little, Brown, 1965. (APRIL — Spring)

Lowry, Lois. *Anastasia Krupnik.* Houghton Mifflin, 1979.
(MAY — Histories)

Maestro, Betsy and Giulio. *Through the Year with Harriet.*
Crown, 1984. (MAY — Yearbooks)

Maestro, Giulio. *Riddle Romp.* Clarion, 1983. (SUMMER — Potpourri)

Maestro, Giulio. *What's a Frank Frank?* Clarion, 1984.
(SUMMER — Potpourri)

Maestro, Giulio. *What's Mite Might?* Clarion, 1986.
(SUMMER — Potpourri)

Marshall, Edward. *Three by the Sea.* E.P. Dutton, 1981. (MAY
— Journals)

Martin, Bill, Jr. *Brown Bear, Brown Bear, What Do You See?*
Holt, Rinehart, & Winston, 1972. (Chapter 1, JANUARY — Animals)

Martin, Bill, Jr. *Silly Goose and the Holidays.* Holt, Rinehart, &
Winston, 1972. (DECEMBER — Holidays)

McCloskey, Robert. *Homer Price.* Viking, 1943. (Chapter 2,
MARCH — Present)

McMillan, Bruce and Brett. *Puniddles.* Houghton Mifflin,
1982. (JANUARY — Winter)

McNulty, Faith. *The Lady and the Spider.* Harper & Row,
1986. (Chapter 2, JANUARY — Animals)

Milne, A.A. *The House at Pooh Corner.* E.P. Dutton, 1928.
(FEBRUARY — Valentine's Day)

Minarik, Else. *Little Bear.* Harper & Row, 1957. (FEBRUARY —
Valentine's Day)

Moerbeek, Kees. *Have You Seen a POG?* E.P. Dutton, 1988.
(JANUARY — Animals)

Montgomery, R.A. *Choose Your Own Adventure: Space and Beyond.*
Bantam Books, 1979. (MARCH — Future)

Morrison, Lillian. *Yours Till Niagara Falls.* Thomas Y.
Crowell, 1950. (MAY — Yearbooks)

Moscovitch, Rosalie. *What's in a Word?* Houghton Mifflin,
1985. (SUMMER — Potpourri)

Most, Bernard. *If the dinosaurs came back.* Harcourt Brace
Jovanovich, 1978. (MARCH — Past)

Noble, Trinka Hakes. *The Day Jimmy's Boa Ate the Wash.*
E.P. Dutton, 1980. (Chapter 1, SEPTEMBER — Field Trips)

Parish, Peggy. *Amelia Bedelia.* Harper & Row, 1963.
(Chapter 1, MARCH — Present)

Parish, Peggy. *Dinosaur Time.* Scholastic, 1974. (MARCH — Past)

Peterson, Scott. *What's Your Name?* Lerner Publications,
1987. (SUMMER — Potpourri)

Renberg, Dalia. *Hello Clouds!* Harper & Row, 1985.
(APRIL — Weather)

Rey, H.A. *Curious George.* Houghton Mifflin, 1941.
(JANUARY — Animals)

Rockwell, Anne. *First Comes Spring.* Thomas Y. Crowell, 1985.
(APRIL — Spring)

Roop, Peter and Connie. *Going Buggy!* Lerner
Publications, 1987. (JANUARY — Animals)

Rounds, Glen. *Ol' Paul The Mighty Logger.* Holiday House, 1936.
(SUMMER — "Reading Rainbow")

Ryder, Joanne. *The Snail's Spell.* Puffin, 1982. (MARCH —
Present)

Rylant, Cynthia. *Birthday Presents.* Orchard Books, 1987.
(MARCH — Present)

Sadler, Marilyn. *Alistair in Outer Space.* Prentice-Hall,
1984. (MARCH — Future)

Sadler, Marilyn. *Alistair's Time Machine.* Prentice-Hall,
1986. (MARCH — Future)

Selsam, Millicent. *How to Be an Animal Detective.*
Scholastic, 1963. (JANUARY — Winter)

Sendak, Maurice. *Chicken Soup With Rice.* Harper & Row,
1962. (MAY — Yearbooks)

Seuss, Dr. *And to Think That I Saw It on Mulberry Street.*
Vanguard Press, 1937. (SEPTEMBER — Field Trips)

Seymour, Peter. *How Things Grow.* E.P. Dutton, 1988.
(APRIL — Growing)

Seymour, Peter. *You Can Be Anything.* Price/Stern/Sloan,
1985. (NOVEMBER — Careers)

Sharmat, Marjorie Weinman. *Gila monsters meet you at the airport.*
Rae Publishing, 1980. (JANUARY — Habitats)

Shaw, Charles G. *It Looked Like Split Milk.* Harper & Row,
1947. (APRIL — Weather)

Sheer, Julian. *Rain Makes Applesauce.* Holiday House,
1964. (APRIL — Weather)

Sleator, William. *Once, Said Darlene.* E.P. Dutton, 1979.
(MARCH — Present)

Slobodkin, Louis. *The Space Ship Returns to the Apple Tree.*
Collier Books, 1958. (MARCH — Future)

Slobodkin, Louis. *The Space Ship Under the Apple Tree.*
Collier Books, 1952. (MARCH — Future)

Slobodkin, Louis. *The Three-Seated Space Ship.* Macmillan,
1962. (MARCH — Future)

Small, David. *Imogene's Antlers.* Crown Publishers, 1985.
(Chapters 1 & 2, MARCH — Present)

Sobol, Donald. *Encyclopedia Brown, Boy Detective.*
Scholastic, 1963. (MARCH — Present)

Spier, Peter. *People.* Doubleday, 1980. (JANUARY — Habitats)

Steig, W. *C D B!* Prentice-Hall, 1968. (SUMMER — Potpourri)

Sterne, Noelle. *Tyrannosaurus Wrecks.* Thomas Y. Crowell,
1979. (MARCH — Past)

Strauss, Joyce. *Imagine That!* E.P. Dutton, 1976. (MAY — Journals)

Terban, Marvin. *Guppies and Tuxedos*. Clarion, 1988.
    (SUMMER — Potpourri)

Thomasson, Merry. *Hey, Look at Me! I Can Be*. Merrybooks,
    1979. (NOVEMBER — Careers)

Tresselt, Alvin. *The Mitten*. Lothrop, Lee & Shepard, 1964.
    (JANUARY — Winter)

Turkle, Brinton. *Deep in the Forest*. E.P. Dutton, 1976.
    (SUMMER — Potpourri)

Twain, Mark. *The Adventures of Huckleberry Finn*.
    Scholastic, 1884. (NOVEMBER — Family)

Twain, Mark. *The Adventures of Tom Sawyer*. Scholastic, 1876.
    (NOVEMBER — Family)

Udry, Janice May. *A Tree Is Nice*. Harper & Row, 1956.
    (APRIL — Spring)

Viorst, Judith. *Alexander and the Terrible, Horrible, No Good,
    Very Bad Day*. Atheneum, 1976. (Chapter 1, MARCH — Present)

Waber, Bernard. *Ira Sleeps Over*. Scholastic, 1972.
    (MARCH — Present)

Walton, Rick and Ann. *Dumb Clucks!* Lerner Publications,
    1987. (JANUARY — Animals)

Walton, Rick and Ann. *Something's Fishy!* Lerner
    Publications, 1987. (JANUARY — Animals)

White, E.B. *Charlotte's Web*. Harper & Row, 1952.
    (NOVEMBER — Family, JANUARY — Animals)

Wilder, Laura Ingalls. *Little House in the Big Woods*.
    Scholastic, 1932. (NOVEMBER — Family)

Wilder, Laura Ingalls. *Little House on the Prairie*.
    Scholastic, 1935. (NOVEMBER — Family)

Williams, Vera. *Three Days on a River in a Red Canoe*.
    Greenwillow Books, 1981. (SUMMER — Summer Fun)

Williams, Vera, and Jennifer Williams. *Stringbean's Trip to
    The Shining Sea*. Greenwillow Books, 1988.
    (SUMMER — Summer Fun)

Winslow, Marjorie. *Mud Pies and Other Recipes*. Macmillan,
    1961. (OCTOBER — Halloween)

Wyllie, Stephen, and Anni Axworthy. *The Great Race*. Harper &
    Row, 1986. (SUMMER — Summer Fun)

Zallinger, Peter. *Dinosaurs*. Random House, 1977. (MARCH — Past)

Zelinsky, Paul. *Rumpelstiltskin*. E.P. Dutton, 1986.
    (SUMMER — "Reading Rainbow")

Zolotow, Charlotte. *Do You Know What I'll Do?* Harper &
    Row, 1958. (MAY — Journals)

Zolotow, Charlotte. *I Know a Lady*. Greenwillow, 1984. (Chapter 1)

Zolotow, Charlotte. *Someday*. Harper & Row, 1965.
    (Chapter 1, NOVEMBER — Careers, MAY — Histories)

Zolotow, Charlotte. *Some Things Go Together*. Harper & Row,
    1969. (SUMMER — Potpourri)

CHILDREN'S MAGAZINES

Chick-A-Dee Magazine and *Owl Magazine,* The Young Naturalist
    Foundation, 56 The Esplanade, Suite 306, Toronto, Ontario
    M5E 1A7, Canada.
Highlights, 803 Church St., Honesdale, PA 18341
National Geographic World, 17th & M Streets NW, Washington, DC 20036
Ranger Rick and *Your Big Backyard,* National Wildlife
    Federation, 8925 Leesburg Pike, Vienna, VA 22184-0001
Sesame Street, P.O. Box 55518, Boulder, CO 80322-5518

PUBLISHERS OF CHILDREN'S WRITINGS

Children's Playmate, 1100 Waterway Blvd., Box 567, Indianapolis,
    IN 46206 (ages 5-8) Publishes original poems, jokes, riddles,
    and pictures.
Cricket, Open Court Publishing, 315 5th St., Peru, IL 61354
    (ages 6-12) Publishes letters, poems, stories, and drawings.
Ebony, Jr.! 820 S. Michigan Ave., Chicago, IL 60605 (ages 6-9)
    Especially for black children. Publishes letters, stories, art,
    riddles, poems, and jokes.
Highlights for Children, 803 Church Street, Honesdale,
    PA 18431 (ages 2-11) Publishes letters, stories, drawings,
    and poems.
Jack and Jill, 1100 Waterway Blvd., Box 567B, Indianapolis,
    IN 46206 (ages 8-12) Publishes letters, poetry, and
    drawings.
Stone Soup, P.O. Box 83, Santa Cruz, CA 95063 (ages 5-14)
    Publishes original artwork, stories, and poems.
Young Authors Week, Sponsored by School Book Fair, Inc., 401
    E. Wilson Bridge Rd., Worthington, OH 43085. Book writing
    competition. Publishes one picture book each year.

RECORDINGS

Barduhn, Art, and Pam Johnson. *Our Dinosaur Friends.* American
    Teaching Aids, 1978. (MARCH — Past)
Henson, Jim. *Fraggle Rock.* Cherry Lane Music, 1983.
    "Friendship Song" by Phillip Balsam & Dennis Lee (NOVEMBER — Friends)
Palmer, Hap. *Ideas, Thoughts, and Feelings.* Educational
    Activity, 1973.
    "Things I'm Thankful For" (NOVEMBER — Family)
Palmer, Hap and Martha. *Witches' Brew.* Activity Records, 1976.
    "Witches' Brew" (OCTOBER — Halloween)
    "They Go Together" (SUMMER — Potpourri)
Raffi. *The Corner Grocery Store.* Troubadour Records, 1979.
    "Cluck, Cluck Red Hen" (JANUARY — Animals)
    "Going on a Picnic" (SUMMER — Summer Fun)
Raffi. *Everything Grows.* Troubadour Records, 1987.
    "Everything Grows" (APRIL — Growing)

Raffi. *Singable Songs for the Very Young.* Troubadour Records, 1976.
    "Five Little Pumpkins" Trad. (OCTOBER — Halloween)
    "The More We Get Together" (NOVEMBER — Friends)
    "Brush Your Teeth" Trad. (FEBRUARY — Dental Health Month)
    "I Wonder If I'm Growing" (APRIL — Growing)
Rapaso, Joseph. *Mother Ghost Nursery Rhymes.* Scholastic, 1968.
    (OCTOBER — Halloween)
Reading Rainbow Songs. Music by Steve Horelick, lyrics by
    Dennis Kleinman and Janet Weir. Caedmon, 1984.
    "If I Brought a Dinosaur Home" (MARCH — Past)
Rogers, Fred. *A Place of Our Own.* Small World Enterprises, 1972.
    "I Need You" (NOVEMBER — Friends)
Rogers, Fred. *Let's Be Together Today.* Small World Enterprises,
    1972.
    "Everything Grows Together" (APRIL — Growing)
Rogers, Fred. *Won't You Be My Neighbor?* Mr. Roger's Neighborhood
    Records, 1981.
    "You're Growing" (APRIL — Growing)
Rogers, Fred. *You Are Special.* Small World Enterprises, 1969.
    "You Are Special" (NOVEMBER — Friends)
Rosenshontz. *It's the Truth.* RS Records, 1984.
    "A Good Friend" Rosen, Shontz, & Storey (NOVEMBER — Friends)
Rosenshontz. *Tickles You!* RS Records, 1980.
    "I Wish I Was" Rosen, Shontz & Storey (JANUARY — Animals)
    "Inch by Inch" David Mallett (APRIL — Growing)
Scruggs, Joe. *Abracadabra.* Educational Graphics Press,
    1986.
    "Abracadabra" (SEPTEMBER — School Routines)
    "Justin" Katrina Butler (NOVEMBER — Friends)
Scruggs, Joe. *Deep in the Forest.* Educational Graphics Press,
    1987.
    "Grandmas and Grandpas" Katrina Butler (Chapter 1)
Scruggs, Joe. *Late Last Night.* Educational Graphics Press,
    1984.
    "Please Don't Bring Your Tyrannosaurus to Show and Tell"
    (MARCH — Past)
Scruggs, Joe. *Traffic Jams.* Educational Graphics Press, 1985.
    "Raindrops and Lemon Drops" Trad. (APRIL — Weather)
Sharon, Lois and Bram. *Elephant Show Record.* Elephant Records,
    1986.
    "Elephant Song" Trad. (OCTOBER — Halloween)
    "On a Picnic We Will Go" (SUMMER — Summer Fun)

COMPUTER PROGRAMS

Creative Writing Series, Pelican® Software. Programs such
as *Dinosaur Days™,* 1988, *Monsters and Make-Believe™,* 1987, and
Transportation Transformation™, 1987. (MAY)

Dazzle Draw™, Broderbund Software, 1984. (JANUARY)

Dinosaur Days™, Pelican® Software, 1988. (MARCH)

Delta Drawing™, Spinnaker Software Corporation, 1984. (JANUARY)

Kidwriter Gold™, Spinnaker Software Corporation, 1988.

Koala Pads Plus™ (includes Koala Pad™ and stylus),

Koala Painter™, and *Graphics Exhibitor™,* Koala
Technologies Corporation, 1984. (Chapter 3, JANUARY)

LogoWriter™, Logo Computer Systems Inc., 1986. (JANUARY)

Multiscribe™, StyleWare, 1986. (MAY)

Multiscribe Picture Manager™, StyleWare, 1986. (MAY)

The Newsroom™, Springboard™, 1984. (MAY)

Printmaster Plus™, Unison World, 1987. (Chapter 3, JANUARY)

The Print Shop®, Broderbund Software, 1984, 1986. (Chapter 3, JANUARY)

Stickybear® Printer, Weekly Reader, 1985. (SUMMER)

SuperPrint!™ Scholastic Software, 1987. (Chapter 3, JANUARY)

ADDRESSES OF SOFTWARE COMPANIES:

BRODERBUND SOFTWARE®
17 Paul Drive
San Rafael, CA 94903-2101

KOALA TECHNOLOGIES CORP
2065 Junction Ave.
San Jose, CA 95131

LOGO COMPUTER SYSTEMS INC.
555 W. 57th Street
Suite 1236
New York, NY 10019

PELICAN SOFTWARE
833 Reseda
Northridge, CA 91324

SCHOLASTIC SOFTWARE
730 Broadway
New York, NY 10003

SPINNAKER SOFTWARE CORP
One Kendall Square
Cambridge, MA 02139

SPRINGBOARD SOFTWARE, INC.
7807 Creekridge Circle
Minneapolis, MN 55435

STYLEWARE, INC.
5250 Gulfton, Suite 2E
Houston, TX 77081

UNISON WORLD
Box 3056
Berkeley, CA 94703

WEEKLY READER SOFTWARE
Middletown, CT 06457

Index

BARE BOOK IDEAS

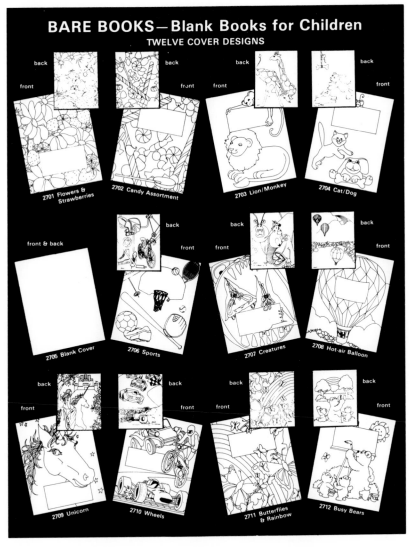

BARE BOOKS—Blank Books for Children
TWELVE COVER DESIGNS

2701 Flowers & Strawberries
2702 Candy Assortment
2703 Lion/Monkey
2704 Cat/Dog
2705 Blank Cover
2706 Sports
2707 Creatures
2708 Hot-air Balloon
2709 Unicorn
2710 Wheels
2711 Butterflies & Rainbow
2712 Busy Bears

For additional information about Bare Books, write to: Treetop Publishing
P.O. Box 085567
Racine, WI 53408

BIG BARE BOOK IDEAS

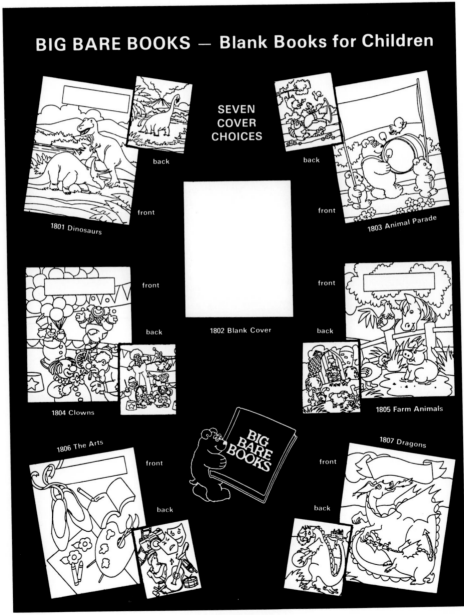

For additional information about BIG Bare Books, write to:

Treetop Publishing
P.O. Box 085567
Racine, WI 53408

Notes

About the Authors

Nancy Oster Steffel taught thirteen years in first grade through high school as a classroom teacher and reading specialist. After receiving her doctorate from Indiana University in 1985, she began teaching reading and language arts methods courses at Butler University in Indianapolis. As a speaker, she gives presentations to parents, teachers, and children on making books and nurturing literacy. In her free time, Nancy loves writing about her family experiences with her husband, Chuck, and her two daughters, Mary (7 years old) and Laura (3 years old).

Susan Griffis Swenson has worked with preschool children and elementary students as a home day-care provider and classroom teacher for more than ten years. In 1981, she received her master's degree in instructional media from Butler University. She presently teaches learning-disabled children at Harcourt Elementary School in Indianapolis. Susie enjoys collaborating with her daughter, Sarah (8 years old), and her husband, Andy, to create their personalized books.

Together, Nancy and Susie write a column, "Parents Nurturing Literacy," and speak at professional conferences on making books with children. To schedule Nancy and/or Susie for a presentation or to share your bookmaking ideas, you may contact them at P.O. Box 90216, Indianapolis, IN 46290-0216.